USING THE SIX ASSETS OF ALIGNMENT
AS THE CATALYST TO IGNITE YOUR LIFE!

ALIGN YOUR EMPIRE

BURTON P. HUGHES

ISBN:
Paperback - 9781954759220
Hardcover - 9781954759237
eBook - 9781954759213

Cranberry Press Publish
Cover design by Clarise Tan
Edited by Hilary Jastram

RESOURCES

IG - Burton_hughes_official

www.burtonhughesofficial.com

TABLE OF CONTENTS

FOREWORD

I've had the privilege and honor of coaching over 20,000 elite people in the last decade. It always intrigues me when I see someone stand out in our busy world by doing the work.

Writing a book is no joke. I know. I've written 13 of them. Number 13 was just as hard, if not harder, than writing number one. So, before I get into it, I want to honor Burton for tapping into his superpower of focus and hammering out a book that will go on to change lives for generations. Congratulations, bro!

Now on to the good part…

I believe that the man who is willing to risk it all on himself is the most powerful man in the room. I'm not talking about gambling, either. I'm talking about men who have moved their families across the country for a commission-only job and made life-changing money. I'm talking about men who have spent their last dime to start a business that has made them millions.

Burton is one of those men. I don't want to spoil the book, but he moved his family to an unknown market, with no guarantee of anything, and no salary. He bet on his skills and work ethic, and his bet paid off.

Burton first came to my office in mid-2019. He requested a meeting with me through one of my sales reps. The sales rep said to me, "This guy is insisting on meeting you. He seems pretty cool; it's probably worth meeting him." So, I had him set up the meeting.

I met with Burton in person at my office a few days later. When he told me his story (which is now in this book), I told him he HAD to write a book about it. Looks like he listened and took action. (Gotta love it!)

After coaching Burton and getting to know him, I encouraged him to spread his experiences and knowledge to a greater base. Because I've seen up close how he performs in life, I want as many people as possible to learn from him.

Burton and I have also partnered on a digital product called The KnockStars, and we actually strapped a GoPro camera to him and sent him to knock on the doors of complete strangers and sell them a roof. I'm telling you, I got it on video—Burton is one of the best ever to do such a challenging chore!

I'm not just Burton's mentor and business partner, though. I'm also one of his best friends. Our kids are even growing up together.

Which reminds me—I'll tell you a story about Burton that definitely won't be anywhere else in this book!

Recently, Burton got a brand new 450 Honda Dirt Bike. He knows my sons and I ride ATVs every weekend, so he asked to go with us on his new bike.

At the park, we suited up and headed out on our bikes. We crossed a creek and rode up some pretty gnarly hills, high above the water below. I made a hard right turn, with my 9-year-old riding his ATV close behind me. As I got around the switchback, I saw Burton and his brand-new bike slide right down the side of the hill. Hell, it hadn't even been cranked for seven minutes! With no hesitation, Burton hopped up, dragged his bike up the hill, and said, "I'm good. Let's go!" What a champion! Nothing deters him! That's Burton.

No setbacks, falls, or slips hold him down.

He popped up with that bike two times as fast as he fell off. That's a serious metaphor for Burton's life and this book. He's the king of bouncing back and landing on his feet quickly.

This book will open your eyes to the possibilities that are right in front of you. As awesome as he is, Burton isn't special: He just puts in the work. And I find that common among those at the top. They aren't necessarily the smartest; they just outwork everyone else. Burton has a proven system he lives by at home and work, and anyone can duplicate it. It's just a matter of actually doing what you need to do.

You're about to read a book that's the true rags-to-riches story about a kid with dreams who grew up to be a man who simply checks off items on his bucket list.

The last thing I'll say is this: After you finish this book, share Burton's story. Put it on social media. Buy another copy of the book for a friend or co-worker. Help him spread the inspiration in this book that you're about to feel.

Rise above,

Ryan Stewman
Entrepreneur

WHAT 3 THINGS DO YOU WANT TO IMPROVE IN YOUR LIFE?

That question is the first thing I ask an audience when I speak at an event.

I ask this because, at any one time, most of us know exactly what we would like to change in our lives. But we usually don't do anything about it.

Answering this question is simple. But people make it complicated. The majority of them focus on what's wrong in their lives rather than what is right.

As you read this book, I encourage you to keep your answers close.

You are about to prime your mind to go after what you want and change what you don't like. And you will need to be strategic to get after it. There is no other choice.

You are about to find your purpose and reinvigorate your life with meaning.

It's not enough to go through your existence without ambition.

I tried it, and 1000/10 of those times, I would not repeat.

Floating through life purposelessly will not get you what you want. You will not have the relationships you want. You will not have the fulfillment you want. You will not have the finances you want. You will not have the business you want.

Thinking that you can treat your existence as a game of hit and miss will undoubtedly set you up for more losses than wins.

(But maybe you already know this?)

Every notable goal has been achieved through purpose. That is why I advise people frequently to do everything with purpose and answer that question. It all ties together and is integral to your success.

Be intentional with your actions. It is the least you can do for yourself.

If your life is lacking purpose, there is really no point in living at all. You are not appreciating the gift you were given and the opportunity to make the best of yourself. This is your responsibility.

Why?

You were put here to live your purpose. It's why you exist. You weren't put here to take up space and never give back.

If you find that statement intimidating, you might be the kind of person who has an excuse ready not to do the work.

But that can't be your true self. You did pick up this book, after all.

If that was you in the past (even if that was you just an hour ago), it's time to shed that version of yourself.

After I share my thought process on igniting your life deliberately, I'm certain your excuses will fall to the wayside.

HOW THE HELL DO I KNOW?

At this point, with very little information about me, you might be thinking, What makes you such an expert, Burton?

I get the skepticism. I also thought that way for a while—back when I was playing small.

So keep that in mind when it seems as if I don't understand your life or what you are dealing with.

By the time you are done reading this book, you will know why I am an expert on blowing up your life the right way.

I also don't teach what I haven't experienced.

For most of my life, I didn't have much of anything. I came from a very humble beginning—one that caused me to hold myself to a higher standard … eventually. But I wasn't like that right off the get-go.

Through those experiences in my background and life, I have worked out how to have it all and ignite my life. And I have even figured out what areas in life to focus on to feel the happiest and become the most fulfilled version of myself. When you are done reading, you will know how to achieve what you want, as well.

(Did you know you hold that potential in your hands right now?)

Having it all in my life came from creating the Six Assets of Alignment. These assets are based on the areas of our lives that we need to keep optimized and operational.

As you read through these pages, I will go deep into where you need to focus and cultivate your time in your Six Assets of Alignment.

For now, allow me to give you a higher overview of what I mean.

THE ART OF STARTING

As you turn the page, start the practice of believing in yourself. This book is about you and how you can change your life and finally get unstuck.

I use these assets as tools to get all the wheels in my life moving in the same direction and supporting the major goal of where I want to be.

I like to think that, to some degree, I have lived my story to help other people. You should know that backing up this book is the real-life example of a person who went after what he wanted—and got it—and that he started out just like you: struggling, searching, doubting, and aimless. That is why I am sharing my story with you in a later part of this book. I believe you need that frame of reference, that my scars give my words credibility. Since you are reading my words, I also think I owe it to you to be real about where I came from.

But my history doesn't matter, and neither does yours.

As soon as I discovered the Six Assets of Alignment, my life changed quickly and to such a degree that I almost couldn't recognize myself.

I use these Six Assets every day to govern my life and keep me in alignment. Without them, I would go off the rails.

SIX KEY AREAS

The Six Assets of Alignment work because they are designed for your modern-day reality. They do not position you to think that there is something wrong with your life, as striving to hit a work-life balance does. The work-life balance forces you to think about the problem and not the solution. When you think about a "work-life balance," it is overwhelming because some part of you believes you cannot do it. Another part of you has to think there is something wrong with the way you are living your life to even consider attempting that kind of balance. You know you will be giving up areas of your life that you don't want to. You might actually resent hoping to hit the work-life balance. You might also fear that the people close to you will resent it, too—because, at some point, they will be holding the short end of the stick when you spend more time at work since you'd neglected it when you were trying to increase quality family time. Use the Six Assets of Alignment, and you will never play catch up!

The Six Assets of Alignment acknowledge what is possible and what isn't. They are your checks and balances and your control. Everything else is variable. As you'll read shortly, when I was in the darkest place in my life, I clung to my fitness. It allowed me to have control and was the glue holding all the broken fragments of my life together. During that time, I learned when you feel good, you look good. You need to make sure that your machine is running in top condition—your body and your mind must be optimal. Your mindset must be focused, or your physical condition will decline—then your work will suffer, and your confidence, money, and relationships will suffer, too.

In the Six Assets of Alignment, you'll focus on:

- Being intentional and deliberate with your time.

- Becoming aerodynamic in reaching your goals—there will be fewer barriers holding you back from reaching them. You might even feel like the universe is conspiring *for* you!

- Accepting the knowledge that balance is a myth and that you truly can finally control your life. With this approach, you will already feel positive about what you are about to implement.

- The only areas of life that matter—knowing that there are more considerations than there have been in the past—when you were growing up and before life became so complicated. Now, we juggle everything! So, let's not fool ourselves; let's just get after it!

- Scheduling time to work on what's important to you, what fuels your life, and is necessary to keep you going successfully every day.

- Seeing more clearly where you need to apply additional resources. You'll start buying back your time and will appreciate that time is the new currency. When it comes to maximizing time, you have to find what works for you, and it will be different for everyone. Some people thrive on working from home amid all the distractions of kids and chaos, and others need to carve out quiet spaces to get their stuff done. It's up to you to figure out what you need. Saving time is similar to preserving your health. You can't plan to get to it later. Use time-blocking where needed, and make sure what you're doing is dollar productive.

Tomorrow will take care of itself if you get done today as much as you can. But if you are not checking all the boxes daily, then you can't hold yourself accountable. And if you don't do what you know you should, how can you continually reevaluate where you're at to ensure you are making progress? This means asking yourself whether where your focus is right now, matters right now. Is what you're doing integral to the business? Are you on the phone when you are supposed to be with your kids?

If one of these Six Assets is neglected, my world crumbles because they are interconnected. I don't want that to happen to you, so please pay attention to each of these critical areas.

The Essence of the Six Assets of Alignment

1. Mindset – **Learn to access powerful mindset control and reject feeling out of control, every day.**

2. Faith – **Tap into your core confidence while feeling the reassurance of a higher power, every day.**

3. Family – **Choose memorable moments that shape your relationships, every day.**

4. Fitness – **You deserve to look and feel your best, every day.**

5. Finances – **Practice smart money management that leads to more money to manage, every day.**

6. Network – **Fill your life with people of substance while rejecting toxic people, every day.**

ASSETS OVERVIEW

MINDSET

Everything you are about to undertake is balanced on mindset. This is the man or woman behind the curtain, controlling every action you take. It informs you on how you feel about yourself, the work you are doing, your faith in yourself, and the pace of your forward momentum. It is for this reason that we will spend most of our time on this Asset.

FAITH

There is a reason that negative posts on Facebook don't receive as much attention by people—or even in the Facebook algorithm! People need hope! Hope is easier to come by when we have the faith that life is going to turn out all right. Faith is relieving and gives us a sense of lightness. We don't need to understand every step in the plan. Our thoughts can rest on faith and knowing we don't have to worry so much.

FAMILY

A.k.a., your rock—a family of blood or your chosen family, it doesn't matter. You need people who love you and who you love back. You need to know as you go through life that you play roles of importance in people's lives, and they in yours. True family is a blessing and is irreplaceable.

FITNESS

Your body holds your soul. You need to love it. You need to get tough with yourself about what you allow so you can break through into the healthiest version of yourself in mind and flesh. Look, life is a dog sometimes. If you want to overcome and be ready to fight, you have to train for it.

FINANCES

Mismanagement of money can feel like a rock around your neck while you're trying to swim. Or it can be the life raft carrying you across the water. At the simplest level, money is a tool that you can use to reach every dream on your vision board or in your head. But the first step you need to take is respecting it. If you want more of it, you can't dislike it and subconsciously drive it away.

NETWORK

Welcome to networking with purpose! So many people believe that they are out there "working the room" when, in actuality, they are just hanging out. They are merely growing their contacts. They are not forging relationships based on commonalities. Too many people forego networking altogether because it makes them feel awkward. We must take imperfect action every day to fill our circle with valuable people we can also pour into.

This won't be the last time you read "Your network is your net worth," because it's true. It matters who you spend your time with. No matter the relationship, your associates must bring value to it. I'm not talking about hanging out with guys or gals and getting wasted. You might have different friends for different purposes in your life. I want to be around people whose values match mine. So I joined a car club. I do business with friends. My chosen family became my brothers and sisters. And we are all resolved to make each other's lives better every day.

THE TOUGHEST QUESTIONS ARE COMING

Before I get into this next part, I want to warn you that, as you read on, I am going to ask you some tough questions. I will inquire about your intentions regarding decisions you have made for yourself and other people, including your closest family. I do this because you cannot reach the level of attainment you want unless you understand where you've come from. In short, you can't have it all unless you do the hard, mental work to get there and apply the Six Assets of Alignment to ensure that you will.

That said, I've worked with people to help them figure out what they've wanted the most for years. There isn't a section of my clients' thought processes that I don't dive into. I leave no fragment of their personality alone. As a coach, it would be irresponsible to do otherwise. I am charged with helping my clients figure out their intentions, their goals, their strategies, and with redirecting them when they don't feel right and don't pay off.

Now, might I also be so bold as to state that I know you are not satisfied with your life right about now? If you were, this book would still be on the shelf, or it wouldn't be on your e-reader.

YOUR STORY

It's time to change your story, and, consequently, your life—to reverse engineer your childhood dreams so you can have what you've been dreaming about.

So you can get out of settling for anything less than those dreams.

If you can't clearly define dreams, you can't work toward them. You might do the work, but you'll have no idea what the goal is, or what your work means. Are you focusing on trying to like the work, on making a game out of moving the goalpost? This is a hell of a trap to try and escape—and sometimes you don't even know that you are in the trap!

We all know the thrill of living for the climax—it's the "what next?" syndrome. You get married, but what next? When are you having kids? When will you buy a house, a new car, go after that promotion? All of these events fill you with expectant dopamine thrills, but what comes after each of them?

Or maybe you hit a significant goal, and now you're terrified, thinking, What the hell did I do that for? Now, I have to prove to myself and everyone else that I can do it again. It can be an ever-repeating cycle of dread.

Maybe you're a person who fixates on the planning. You can't stop poring over all the steps you need to take—and you never actually take them.

There are so many ways that we pigeonhole ourselves against success.

Everyone has the want and the desire, but we often get confused. If you're procrastinating, you might really be a perfectionist. Do you see yourself in the following scenario—

Are you stuck trying to calculate the ROI when, if you took less-than-perfect action, you could progress a good deal farther?

Use these Six Assets, and you can finally have it all.

You'll want to give everything you can to the people closest to you.

You'll appreciate everything and want for nothing.

You'll rewrite the messages you tell yourself.

Doesn't erasing "can't" from your vocabulary and viewing your life as a limitless gift sound incredibly marvelous?

I promise you, the process you are about to read about and experience is not the least bit intimidating. There's nothing to memorize, even.

There's just you, giving yourself a shot to use what worked for me so you can thoroughly impact and improve your life.

Let's do this together.

Before you move on to the next page, I invite you to start thinking about these several everyday things you can do to improve your life in every area of the Six Assets of Alignment:

1. Mindset: Read ten pages of a motivational book every day.

2. Faith: Create time to give thanks daily.

3. Family: Time-block your kid's games, so you don't double book yourself.

4. Fitness: Reduce the amount of dessert you put on your plate.

5. Finances: Stop the panic of slashing expenses and rationing money; resolve to get comfortable with making more of it. Get on offense!

6. Network: Keep your promise to deepen your network by connecting with people who are where you want to be a year from now.

These are just a few simple suggestions to inspire you to think bigger and follow through.

Once you've explored what more you can do, go ahead and turn the page. It's time to prepare yourself for living in Alignment with your 6 Assets.

SECTION 1:
THE SIX ASSETS OF ALIGNMENT

THE MAJOR POINTS OF THE SIX ASSETS OF ALIGNMENT

"To achieve great things, two things are needed:
a plan, and not quite enough time."
—Leonard Bernstein

I named my program the Six Assets of Alignment because maximizing these six key areas of your life will provide you with the highest value of anything you do.

Again, these are the six key areas of your life that are the most critical to keep in alignment:

1. Mindset

2. Faith

3. Family

4. Fitness

5. Finances

6. Network

None of them is greater than any of the others. They're all equally important. The goal is to get them all working in top form simultaneously.

Identifying and then doubling down my focus on these six Assets has brought me more intimate and meaningful relationships, peace of mind, improved physical fitness, financial stability, a luxury lifestyle, spiritual oneness, and reassurance.

The alignment of these assets also allows me to keep leveraging all my blessings so I will keep leveling up in life.

While building each of the six Assets, the most important thing to remember is that they all work in tandem.

[**When you are successful with one asset, you will be successful with them all.**]

When you are successful with one Asset, you will be successful with them all.

WHY ALIGNMENT WORKS OVER BALANCE

Balance is a myth!

As I noted before, the problem with the work-life balance theory is that it's impossible to do. One area or another is always going to suffer. Subscribe to the work-life balance theory, and you will take energy from your business and add it to your family to get the scale to balance, but that means your business ultimately ends up lacking. When you switch back to more of a business focus, your family then feels a loss. Ultimately, you just end up feeling torn and spread too thin. No one area of your life wins.

Maybe that's why everyone writes about it. No one can figure it out. It just doesn't work.

Balance is impossible.

So, let's get these areas working together instead of fighting to make them balanced.

Here's an example: When I'm in my home office, my door is closed, and my kids know that Daddy's working. But if they need me, I'm available. When I'm out on appointments, and I come home, I hear, "Daddy, did you have a good appointment?"

Alignment is very much intertwined in my day. Everything points in the same direction. As I do well with my business, I've been able to take care of my family. That's why my daughter can ask without resentment how my day went when I return home to her.

You'll find your own rhythm as you work to align your life. Eventually, everything will work in harmony, and then you'll do it again. But keep in mind, the Six Assets of Alignment are *not* a routine—it's **caretaking of all these focused areas of your life at the same time.** It's you, practicing integrity in every one of these areas.

When you do that, you're working for good and doing everything you can possibly do. You're practicing your ethics while staying true to your core principles. Your faith is in line because you're taking care of your family because your business is taken care of. Your finances are handled because your business is killing it because you are networking well. It's a beautiful, cyclical situation. Your goals in every area are aligned to ensure you elevate your life. The way you parent feeds into the type of person you want to be—a person you'll feel proud of. The way you budget your money allows you to live as the person you strive to be. Think of the Six Assets of Alignment as a light illuminating forward and lighting up a big target. But the target is the highest version of yourself. If anything is out of sequence, if any light points in a different direction or any goal strays from your strongest intention, you cannot achieve being the person you want to become— who you know you are meant to be.

If I have a goal to scale my business, but I refuse to seek out clients, I am out of alignment in the Network Asset. Whatever goal I set, each asset supports.

If I have a goal to be more present with my children but make an excuse not to take them to the zoo as we had planned, I am out of alignment in my Family Asset.

Every asset is defined for my highest purpose. Keeping my actions congruent, or clicking together, means whatever I do serves my highest aim or goal.

You can use the Six Assets of Alignment to conquer anything you want in life.

For ten years, I thought I was doing the right thing and climbing that ladder of success, but my ladder was on the wrong wall, as Thomas Merton has said.

I have literally crashed and burned in each of these six areas, and so I am well aware of what works (and what doesn't) from experience. I've had faith. I've lost faith. I've made a lot of money and lost a lot of money—all because I was self-centered and not centered on Alignment.

I had to realize that God has given me the tools I need for every opportunity.

1. Mindset: I crashed and burned when I wasn't inputting good, positive information into my brain daily. Your brain is a muscle to exercise daily.

2. Faith: I crashed and burned when I drifted from God and the gifts He has given me.

3. Family: I crashed and burned when I allowed the pain of my childhood to legitimize my excuses to be distant from the people I loved.

4. Fitness: I crashed and burned when I wasn't focused on taking care of my body.

5. Finances: I crashed and burned when I sold myself short and accepted a salaried job because it was comfortable—even though it killed my entrepreneurial spirit.

6. Network: I crashed and burned when I discounted the influence and positivity of the people I wanted to be around.

These low moments in my life have everything in common. I may have crashed and burned, but I came back when I put the Six Assets of Alignment to work for me all at the same time.

WATCH PRIDE AND EGO

Remember, as you go forward, that pride and ego are a delicate balance. Accept that you will need a healthy ego and remember there is a reason for the old saying, "Pride goeth before a fall." It is possible to have too much of a good thing! Think about the influencers you see on Instagram and Facebook. Maybe you've noticed how active they were in posting, only to fall off and grow silent when they lose it all? Don't forget what the true greats do! They don't care much about the perceptions of others. They live by the values that mean something to them to lead them in their best direction.

[
I keep myself in line through one of my mantras: "Ego is what makes you good. But humility is what makes you great."
]

I keep myself in line through one of my mantras: "Ego is what makes you good. But humility is what makes you great."

God put me on earth for a reason. He put you on earth for a reason. Your moral compass keeps you on your chosen path. We are all given gifts, and it's up to us to live up to them or not. Keep in mind that true God-given gifts are not meant to place you in shady areas—working dirty business deals, being unfaithful in relationships, etc. These gifts are meant to keep you successful in the light. Stay true to that moral compass (you'll sleep better at night, I promise!). I teach the Six Assets of Alignment because anytime I've tried to live out of alignment, I've had the most turmoil.

All the self-help books have the same kind of premise, but I have a different way of approaching it. I like to consider myself your Chief Reminding Officer. I want to remind you of the six areas where you need to focus to make your life better, consistently, every day for the rest of your life.

When you use the Six Assets of Alignment, you will get back on the offense— you will live every moment of your life intentionally. You will take more risks that make more sense.

For instance, at the start of the COVID-19 pandemic, I didn't necessarily know where I was going. But I knew I was in the right setting and that I had the fortitude to see it through. I was very self-assured. I wasn't careless, but I took calculated risks—anything to take care of my family.

YOU *CAN* BE WEALTHY AND RELIGIOUS / SPIRITUAL

If you are holding yourself back because you believe the Bible indicates you shouldn't be wealthy, I want you to know that the Bible talks more about money and being a good steward in business than anything else. It's an absolute myth that you need to deprive yourself. Understand, it's not money that's the root of evil—it is the worship of money, known as "mammon."

When you think of money as an entity, realize that's where the devil lies.

Additionally, it's vital to remember that we are called upon to use money for good. As I have stated, the more successful you are, the more you can give back.

God wants you to be prosperous. How many times in the Bible did He make people kings? Many kings shared their fortune to benefit others. This is an example you can follow to alleviate any guilt as you enjoy the warmth that comes into your heart from acting in benevolence. Do good things with your money to help change the world for the better and forget this misconception. Then see the opportunities that come for you and be ready to seize them. Work toward being in a place where you can receive opportunities and turn them into favors for both you and others.

INSIST ON EXCELLENCE

Louis Pasteur said, "Chance favors the prepared mind." That means you should assert excellence in everything you do.

Ask yourself, honestly, How am I showing up?

My gifts were intimidating to me when I was younger. (They were even more intimidating to the people around me.) I think that was part of the reason that I ran from them for so long. Maybe you think you can't accept your gifts because if you do, people won't like you.

If that's the case, then how can you fully accept and like yourself? I want you to embrace all of your gifts to their fullest and live in excellence. Don't apologize for who you are or what you bring to the table. Appreciate your gifts. Hone your gifts. Get accustomed to demanding excellent standards of yourself and others.

Think about, How am I giving back? What is my purpose? Where am I making excuses so I can keep playing small?

FREEDOM FROM THE DARKNESS

The following section and sections beyond contain references to suicide and suicidal ideation. Please don't read them if you are struggling in this area. Get help through the National Suicide Prevention Lifeline: 800-273-8255.

When I started using the Six Assets of Alignment every day, I finally didn't feel like an alien. All my life, I've felt like the only person who didn't fit in. I couldn't say the right words, didn't look the right way, and didn't live the way other people did.

I feel so alive now, so good and free, as if I deserve everything I have in my life—because I do!

I've never shared this before, but when I was younger, I contemplated suicide a lot.

After I left home, my life was not one big ascent upward. It was more of a roller coaster ride. Needless to say, life didn't get better instantly.

I made mistakes.

I got divorced.

I lost money.

I lost people.

I doubted myself and made horrible decisions, and I certainly didn't treat myself as if I loved myself.

Sometimes, we can get absolutely exhausted from thinking too much. That was definitely the case when I was forging out on my own.

My dad told me once that when I was younger, I was insatiable. To this day, I think about his statement and whether or not what he had seen when I was just a kid was connected to my drive, and whether or not he meant it as an insult.

> *All I know is this is my makeup. I have control over it, but I don't.*

All I know is this is my makeup. I have control over it, but I don't.

CHOOSING MYSELF / CHOOSING YOURSELF

Even as a kid, I wondered what it would be like to be dead. As an adult, fresh out of the trailer park, I took out insurance policies on myself and put them in my mom's name. My plan was to work for a couple of years so she would be set;

then, when I offed myself, the policy wouldn't be in question. That's really how I thought and almost planned out my whole life—which would have been a very short time on this planet.

Until I saved myself.

Until I chose myself.

Until I started living differently.

I've put a gun to my head and felt that cold steel on my temple. I can't begin to tell you the moment of clarity I received in that moment. Just as I've heard, "That's not for you," my whole life, I knew that dying wasn't for me, either. That cold steel woke me up.

I truly did not want to die. I have never wanted to die. I just wanted a solution.

But this time, I made the right decision to live differently. It was either that, or I would die.

I can tell you, instead of wishing the pain away, there is a far more effective solution.

Before we move on, I do want to reiterate that if you are feeling like a danger to yourself, get help. There's no shame in that. Sometimes, we need help, and when we are on firmer ground, then we can pursue a new regimen and way of life.

I got into a place where I could commit to living a certain way every day.

If you are ready, let's put these assets to work for you and apply them to your life.

MINDSET

Let me be clear: If you are reading this book and thinking it will directly lead you to a nice, cozy promotion and that it will make you set for life—this book is not for you. If you are of the mind to settle for the nine-to-five and the daily grind when what you really want is that laptop lifestyle, you are not being honest with yourself. Until you can be, you won't be happy.

> *Let me be clear: If you are reading this book and are thinking it will directly lead you to a nice, cozy promotion and that it will make you set for life— this book is not for you.*

I can't make it any more plain or simpler than that.

I can't relate to you more than sharing that I have also walked a rutted and worn-down road and now float along in a Rolls-Royce across the smoothest blacktop. It's an analogy, but it's also real-life.

In case you need more convincing, here's another true, staggering statistic that came right out of my life.

I didn't have role models in high school. The administration sat us down in the auditorium on the first day of school. Six hundred-thirty-five kids were all crammed together. The speaker of the day addressed us and said, "The person on the right and left sides of you will not graduate."

I laughed, but it was true. My senior class only had 152 kids graduate.

In my freshman year, over 40 girls got pregnant and dropped out that same year.

So if you feel that you have a limiting mindset or that you're starting behind the line, I get it. I have been there, and I got the T-shirt (and yearbook) to boot.

> *So if you feel that you have a limiting mindset or that you're starting behind the line, I get it. I have been there, and I got the T-shirt (and yearbook) to boot.*

You might have to do a little more work to move over the hurdles in your mind. But if I can do it, so can you!

I want you to work on this and make controlling your thoughts as much a part of your day as a regular workout. I want you to understand that a healthy mindset is more valuable than any amount of money. You will never reach any financial pinnacles until you get your mindset in shape.

It's impossible unless someone walks up to you and hands you a bunch of cash, but with a crappy mindset, you probably wouldn't attract them or that money—not kidding! If by some long shot, they did that, and you took the cash, you would likely also rush to spend it since you haven't conditioned your mind to manage money.

Most of the time, when people think about the goals they want to attain, they hyper-focus on money. They don't include the more critical pieces of getting there, like believing they can earn a surplus, in the first place.

It makes sense, then, that the top 1% in this country have more assets than all the middle class combined. I'm sure you've actually heard that before, but when you really think about it, isn't that a startling statistic? When you peel it apart, you learn that everything the one-percenters have achieved stems from their mindset. In other words, those at the top of their game know that they can do anything. All they have to do is set their mind to it and do it. The power of their minds doesn't allow them to think they won't reach their goals. They can't fathom not achieving their goals.

This is not blind faith—these people have unwavering faith in themselves.

When they close their eyes, no matter their target, they see it clearly in their mind, like a preview of a winning moment to come.

Possessing and using an empowering mindset means turning on the potential in your mind. It means being intentional and disciplined in what you allow yourself to think and the self-talk you permit.

I have known people who have woken up and decided they've had enough bullshit, and then watched them claim what they wanted in the world.

I have seen people refuse to discover where true confidence lies—within—and it changed the course of their lives, too.

I have witnessed little wins transformed into huge feats, and the people orchestrating them shock themselves as they feel they have unlocked a secret of the universe: how to be abundant.

I am not coming to you as a friend of a friend's mother's dog's stepsister. What I am telling you about, I built with my own two hands. My friends have built their successes with their own hands.

So you will not convince me that you can't do it.

If you don't do it, you only have to stare at yourself in the mirror to see the truth—you are holding yourself back.

Take what I am confiding in you as a key that will unlock all the hidden parts of you that are ready to dominate.

But how do you do this? You must be relentless in turning off negative thoughts. You must practice doing this every day, just like you need to exercise every day. You will need a way to stop yourself from falling down into a spiral, a plan to apply when your mind wants to fight you. Some people teach themselves to shout "No!" in their minds. Some people tell themselves negativity is a lie. The point is to rehearse your plan for what you will do when things get hard. If you have a string of bad days, for instance, how will you correct it? How will you change this bad direction? Everyone is different, and they devise their own alternative solutions. You can try:

1. Meditation

2. Prayer

3. Practicing a bit of NLP (Neuro-Linguistic Programming). When negative thoughts threaten to overtake you, yell an opposing word in your head.

4. Reassure yourself that you know the lies your brain is feeding you aren't true.

5. Take a time out and commit to doing something hard, possibly a fitness challenge or something that pushes your physical ability.

6. Listen to motivational podcasts or audiobooks.

7. If you can't get unstuck, get help! Talk to a therapist or a trusted friend or family member.

FAITH

Faith anchors you to being a good person at your core. I believe whatever I accomplish, I haven't done on my own. Faith means staying on the right path and doing the right thing. I know if I do everything I possibly can today, tomorrow is going to take care of itself. I shared this before, but it's so powerful, it bears repeating.

That's also faith.

As you can see, faith has many sides.

People who come from repeated trauma, exposure to poverty, and long decades of generational pain, seem to run worst-case scenarios in their heads. Because no matter how much you grow, no matter how much you step into your purpose, it is engrained in you. If you can relate to this, you might need to work a little harder to manage your urge to question faith.

Then again, you may have to live with that struggle. If that is the case, it's okay. This is who you became at a formative age. So, is it that you are never going to stop running worst-case scenarios? No. But are you going to get better at living with them? Yes, because when you are conscious of it and work toward improving your experiences, it will get easier—even if it never goes away.

I'm in the middle of what I call divine tension. I am appreciative of my blessings and my life, but I want more.

[*I also have the faith that I will get it—it is meant for me.*]

I also have the faith that I will get it—it is meant for me.

When I was young, I had reduced lunches because we were so poor. My lunches only cost 40 cents. It was humiliating, and I would skip eating because I didn't want people to see me getting reduced tickets. Kids would ask, "Why aren't you eating?" I would say, "I'm just not hungry." But the hunger pains coming out of my stomach, man, I can hear them to this day. It was like an orchestra. That's divine tension. I could eat, but I wanted more.

How to mediate the challenges of faith when you feel you have lost your way and belief in yourself and something more —

1. Understand that God expects your feelings, even your anger. His love never dies.

2. Remind yourself that our greatest trials can produce the most unbreakable faith.

3. Freefall out of control and learn that life isn't as bad as you anticipate (usually).

4. Try keeping things in perspective—not to invalidate what you are going through but reminding yourself that you will choose your problems from a pile of everyone else's will set you straight again.

5. Give thanks that you are self-aware enough to make different decisions.

6. If you can't find belief in yourself, remember you are a product of moments. They are what made you. Embrace it!

7. Look forward to what is coming next. As the saying goes (I have found this to be true, again and again), "It is always darkest before the dawn."

FAMILY

Family should be the center of your life. You can lean on your family in tough times. Please note, I am also including your family of choice under the definition of "family." I have my blood family, but I also have my family of choice, who are my true brothers, and the people that I've chosen to live life with.

In my family, I integrate being a father and provider as a major priority. Often, fathers are portrayed as fumbling, overweight idiots. Believe it or not, dads have the ability to do the same things moms can do. You can take your kids to the car wash or run errands. You can take them to their doctor appointments. Whatever it might be, wherever you are needed, you, as a dad, are capable. You simply have to make the choice—step up and be the parent you always wanted. For so many of us (men and women alike), it's really about being the parent we needed as a child.

When I'm spending time with my family at night, we'll watch a show together. I will read to my daughters before bed. When I was in kindergarten, my stepmom helped me with my reading because I had such a hard time. What's sad is that's truly the only memory I have of anyone reading with me. So, I make time for my kids. I want them to have lots of memories to pick from. It makes me feel more involved.

I have a pretty competent business contact that I talk to on a regular basis, but he basically missed the first 15 years of his kid's life because he is self-employed and put his family on the backburner. He's been on this continual grind. I've wanted to say to him, How many games did you miss when all you had to do was show up? Is that the simple shift in mindset or awakening you need, too? Show up. Your kids will remember that you did it.

> *Your children are watching how you talk to their other parent.*
> *How you respect them. How you honor them. How you love*
> *them. They're paying attention to how family life should be.*

Your children are watching how you talk to their other parent. How you respect them. How you honor them. How you love them. They're paying attention to how family life should be.

If you're reading this book and honestly wondering where to start making changes in your life, family is a great place to start!

Mother Teresa said, *"If you want to change the world, go home and love your family."*

Be the man/woman you want to be.

Be the spouse/partner you want to be.

Be the father/mother you want to be.

When you struggle to align your family values, try the following:

1. When you are arguing, back down. Offer to listen first, help the other person first, extend a kind gesture to them.

2. Ask your partner or the person you are fighting with how they really feel and ensure them that you will only listen.

3. Recognize that sometimes the relationships we want the most that require the most time can be very unexciting: hauling the kids here and there, grocery shopping, bills, etc. It's unglamorous, and it's supposed to be.

4. Change your situation. Don't go to your usual restaurant. Hit the beach for the day instead. Take a writing class with your spouse or an older child. Make a space family-friendly in your home or outside it, so you can all gather in comfort. There are even a few apps that you can download that are like flashcard challenges that ask serious/funny and some introspective questions to make you grow closer in your relationship.

5. Stop and pray together.

6. Take responsibility for your actions and words, and resist being defensive.

FITNESS

If you're going to be a high performer, you need to be mentally and physically fit. If you're not, it's time to get there.

Before I made working out and taking care of my body a way of life, I had low self-esteem, and fitness helped me with that.

Fitness allowed me to build more than my physical stature.

[*Fitness allowed me to build more than my physical stature.*]

It made me work on my routine and conditioned my mind to be strong and resilient. I had to work in the gym, day in and day out, and completely quit drinking to become better at lifting and improving my health.

When I was working in new home sales and the mortgage industry in my twenties, I felt pretty good about myself. I was making good money, but I lacked a desired level of confidence. As I told you, I was a scrawny kid growing up and was only about 40 pounds soaking wet in the fourth grade. So, I decided to join a gym to get in shape. Hopefully, then I would gain that elusive confidence I'd been grasping for. Then I would have that body. Boom. I thought I had my plan all figured out and that it would be easy. But like every other person out there that embarks on a fitness journey without any real plan or change in mindset, I fizzled out in only a few short weeks.

It was another five years before I could really commit to fitness and pursue bodybuilding with a vengeance. It was only when I channeled my focus and fortified my mindset that I became unstoppable—to the point it nearly led to my downfall.

THE BUILDING OF THE BODY

Once I convinced myself that I was ready to work on my physique for real, I shared my fitness goals and plan to get into shape with my boss one day. When I did, all I heard in between a few short chuckles was, "You don't have the bone structure for that."

Damn. That hurt.

Hearing that I wasn't going to achieve my dreams stopped me cold. I felt like that little trailer park boy with the big dreams who had been told to sit down, shut up, and dream smaller. That day a fire was reignited inside me (for both my present self as well as that kid from the West Side.) I decided to get a trainer and dietician because I knew I couldn't do it on my own.

In the fall of 2009, I hired the best personal trainer in Ohio. He was known as the guy who could take "normal" people and turn them into professional bodybuilding athletes. It cost me a bunch of money, but my mindset was right; I was seriously committed and ready to invest in myself.

I really wasn't looking to be a competitive bodybuilder. I just wanted to get in great shape. I'd worked for Abercrombie & Fitch when I was 18 (you've seen the guy on the bags with the swimmer body—that was me). Now, I just wanted a little more meat on my bones and not to feel undersized, to be more muscular and feel more confident.

When I met the trainer, I told him: "I need your help." He replied, "Here's what we're gonna do. You're fit right now, but we're going to have to get you fat so that we can add muscle to your frame. That means you're gonna go from fit to fat, then from fat to fit." He must've seen the confused look on my face because he explained that I had to get fat to get to an anabolic state to build muscle.

I paused for a minute and said, "Sounds terrible—I'm in!" Then I shook his hand.

Over the next few months, I put on 50 pounds eating flank steak, sweet potatoes, and cans of cherry and apple pie filling. I was large. I didn't check my sugar back then, but I wouldn't doubt if I was pre-diabetic.

I remember trying to show homes and struggling walking up flights of stairs because I was so heavy. I would point to the upper level and say to my clients with a forced smile, "Second-floor laundry. Go ahead and check it out. I'm walking back downstairs and will meet you folks there."

It was that bad. But it was part of the plan. And I was committed.

It's funny to think back on my first day of training in November 2009. I would have said the goal was to get me in shape for the summer. I never set out to be a bodybuilder; I just wanted some confidence. But there was a bodybuilding show scheduled for the middle of May.

The words bodybuilder and fitness professional have a negative stigma.

At the time, I was working so hard to win in all the competitions, that negative stigma hurt me. I reeled from the counterculture.

Bodybuilder is synonymous with jock, muscle builder, muscleman, etc. Those terms only cheapen the hard work and dedication that goes into the sport.

Let me explain …

You've heard what happens when people decide to get into serious physical shape. Here comes the peanut gallery, a.k.a. the other people who don't want to hold themselves to a higher standard. These people can get super uncomfortable because the work you're doing shines a light on the work they are not doing. A lot of people around me tried to break my spirit.

One day in early January 2010 (and in front of everybody), my trainer announced, "Hey guys! Burton Hughes is going to do his first show in May!" The people around him all said, "Oh man, that's awesome!" Everyone seemed so excited for me. Even proud.

He glanced at me and asked, "How do you feel about that?"

I answered that I felt great. Inside, I wasn't as confident. My plan was to simply follow the path I was paying someone to lay out for me. Then I hoped the confidence would come. I knew what I wanted and that I would work to achieve it. My mindset was right.

When my trainer told me, "We have to get you fat," I was on board. I'm coachable that way. I wanted it more than I wanted to fight him on what I thought I should do.

All too often, we let our ego get in the way of tough goals. We hire somebody to be our coach, when what we're really looking for is just to have someone agree with us. In my opinion, coachability has to be one of the most vital and intangible assets an individual can have. I hear a lot, "I'm coachable," but people aren't always willing to unlearn what they think they know. Only once the ego has stepped aside can one truly learn, grow, and achieve.

[
I actually look forward to the miserable work that needs to be done to rise to the levels I want to be on.
]

What I've learned about myself over the years is that I really enjoy being coached;

I like to be uncomfortable. I actually look forward to the miserable work that needs to be done to rise to the levels I want to be on.

I approached my fitness that way back then, and I still have the same attitude.

Over those next five months, I lost 64 pounds and got into the best shape of my life. I was going to do the bodybuilding show!

I was doing everything to stay on track to achieve my goal.

In the middle of May 2010, I got on the scale and made the weight goal set for me. Following the recipe was working. The next day, I took third place in my very first bodybuilding competition. Anyone else would have been happy to get that slot. I was sick to my stomach.

I didn't sleep all weekend after the competition because my mind was on a loop of constantly thinking: Why the hell should I do anything if I'm not going to win? I play to win. I don't just run the bases.

I was in the best shape of my life and got third place. But I was pissed. I'd lost sight of the goal.

That's my mindset.

I can be brutal. There's a darker side to having such a forceful drive. It can be perceived as negative because you're never satisfied. You always want more.

But because I am wired the way I am, I could stop and take a breath.

I could figure out what I wanted and refocus to get my mind right.

In my head, I was still the young, undersized kid who wanted to win. I hadn't proved I was any different than that child, and it felt like I had made zero progress from wanting to escape my childhood—all because I hadn't won.

What a kick to the dick!

That following Monday, I walked into the gym, still in a foul mood.

That's when I ran into an old-time bodybuilder, Jack Ellers. He was in great shape, and just like a real modern-day Mr. Miyagi, Jack took one look at my sour face and snapped, "What's the matter with you? You're not happy with the way you placed?"

I scowled back at him and said, "No, I'm pissed about it." He pressed me. "When's your next show?"

I told him I had a short 21 days to take first.

Jack asked, "How many meals do you eat a day?"

"Five meals and two snacks."

"How many cardios daily?"

"Two a day."

"How many times do you weight train per day?"

"One."

His face looked like he had just bitten into a fresh lemon after I answered all his questions. He stuck a finger in my chest and said, "You mean to tell me you can't get better in 147 meals, 42 cardios, and 21 workouts?"

My mind was blown. (***Major*** mindset adjustment here!)

All this time, I had been thinking about 21 days and how that felt like such a short period of time, but Jack broke it down to an easily attainable goal. My thinking had been ridiculous (and small)—his made so much more sense.

After this life-altering attitude adjustment, I went on to win many bodybuilding competitions, eventually turning pro in the division of Men's Physique. It seems I did have the bone structure for this weightlifting stuff, after all.

Keep in mind that fitness is so much more than aesthetics. I recently had a heart scan, and the results showed I have zero blockage. At the age of 38, I am extremely healthy. I don't smoke cigarettes. I choose not to drink alcohol. In my family, people have cirrhosis of the liver by the time they're middle age. Some family members are on drugs. Addiction is in my genes. I don't want any of that, and when you take a step back and look at the big picture, I'm sure you don't either.

Twenty years from now, I want to walk my daughters down the aisle. I'll be able to hop, skip, and jump down that aisle if I want to because of how I take care of myself. And I will be able to! No doubt in my mind.

Being physically fit gets me more business, too—because I'm more confident, but I also work hard at it. It's not only my body but every area of my life that I keep fit. You can eat off the floor of my truck. People see that, and they say, "I know he's gonna do a good job, no matter what." The old saying is that you can't judge a book by its cover, but I like to add that a good book cover can give you a pretty good idea of what you're dealing with.

Getting back into alignment with your Fitness Asset is easiest when you take emotion out of it and follow these steps:

1. Make a plan to go to the gym. Then go. If you don't know what machines to work on or what classes to attend, consult a trainer.

2. Incentivize working out by allowing yourself to revel in the most enjoyable aspects of it. If you need to, reward yourself when you're done. Always remember: Do the things you have to do so you can do the things you want to do. A funny thing will happen along the way, and those tough workouts will actually become something you enjoy when you learn to embrace them! Trust me when I say you'll be better for it!

3. Share your experience with another person. Your best friend, your sister, brother, a close neighbor—bring them along. Older kids *love* to go to the gym. You just may be the catalyst they need to start their own fitness journey!

4. Not a chef? No problem. I rely on healthy meals delivered to my home that eliminate my excuses to eat unhealthily. There are so many tools available for you to attain your health goals!

5. Get a little vain. A huge feeling of accomplishment sweeps over you when you start to improve your body, when muscles peek out from under fluff. You earned it! Go ahead and stare at those abs and glutes!

6. Try new recipes! Have you been wanting to go gluten-free, dairy-free, to drink a green smoothie every day for breakfast? Do it! Just find what works for you and stick with it!

7. Make it a game! How fast can you go? How many new exercises can you try? How much can you lift? Daily challenges are a fun way to mix up your workouts to help push through fitness plateaus.

FINANCES

Finances are your grind. They are your work, your bottom line. Of course, you need to be proficient and efficient here.

Believe me when I tell you it doesn't matter if you're a janitor or a CEO. Devote yourself to being the best, and people will take notice.

I'll work the hardest, the longest, and the most efficiently.

I'll read the books.

I'll pay the money to go to the mastermind gatherings. I will literally do anything (as long as it's morally sound) to gain an edge.

All of the above feeds into having more skills—which equals more money.

The Finances Asset was really the first area in my life where I felt confident. And maybe it was easier to hit my targets there because I knew I only had to perform, and I would get there. I know I follow through on what I say, and when I do that, I make a difference.

Right before I got into new home sales, I went out and played a game of darts with the guys. One of them was bragging about their lack of a schedule and how much money they were making. I learned there was an opportunity to slide into that industry because one of the dude's assistants hadn't shown up for work. So, the following day, I put on a shirt and tie, went to this guy's office, and told him, "I'm coming to work for you."

This boss man shot me an expression like: "Who the hell are you?" I'm sure he was thinking, *You're not female. You're not blonde. No.*

> *The problem with finances is when you're no longer hungry, and you have a roof over your head, and you have a car, and cell phone, etc., you get comfortable and settle in because all your basic needs are met.*

I said, "Your assistant is taking this opportunity for granted." He sat back in his chair and stared at me like I had horns growing out of my head. I stared right back and said, "I'm not taking no for an answer. I'll work here for free, but I'm coming to work for you." He hired me on the spot, and the rest is history. My tenacity turned into a super nice payoff!

But the problem with finances is when you're no longer hungry, and you have a roof over your head, and you have a car, and cell phone, etc., you get comfortable and settle in because all of your basic needs are met.

When I was young, my father called me insatiable. I learned when I was older that "insatiable" meant I always wanted more. That nothing was ever good enough.

He'd say, "You're not even my son. I don't understand you." That hurt to hear, but it also made me understand myself better. Insatiable is exactly who I am.

Insatiable works very well in the finance game.

In my first major month in roofing sales, I closed roughly $50k in commissions, and it made me even hungrier. I thought, I can become a multi-millionaire by knocking doors? Sign me up for that!

I learned that when I put on my work uniform and performed, I was like everyone else. (Except, if I can humbly say so, I was excellent.) Regardless, I finally fit in. No one knew where I came from. I didn't have to hide myself, and I liked it. Success produced by good, hard work was my new uniform. When I wore it, I was no longer vulnerable. I was in complete control.

Can't figure out finances? Follow these steps:

1. Stop financial self-sabotage. If you've worked hard to scale your business and start earning more, but you're uncomfortable, *stop*! That's right. Do nothing. Buy nothing. Don't justify anything when you feel like this. No new anything. It's not forever, but it is to build a solid habit to hold onto your cash.

2. Don't deny what you want; just live in moderation. Maybe you don't need to eat out every night, but once a week is probably okay.

3. Who cares about keeping up with the Joneses? Your friend got a new supercar. That's got nothing to do with you. Your time is coming, but not when you can't afford it. You'll know when the time is right!

4. One of the ways to make yourself the most resilient is to practice delayed celebration. Train yourself to wait and give yourself reasonable rewards. Maybe something for the house or another golf club.

5. Put your money to work—smartly. If you don't know how to do this, work with a financial advisor. Have someone teach you about real estate investing or stocks.

6. Restrict yourself. Stop spending, and put cash into a savings account that you can't spend. Use a CD or open an E-Trade account to make your money work for you!

NETWORK

Networking connects you to people and what you want to do, what you are working on. I always try and link the two. Life is more enjoyable that way, and my networking is more successful when I link to people with that in mind.

I've joined car clubs and met people at the gym to grow my circle. You can do the same thing. Think about your business, hobbies, and what you like to do, and then make a concerted effort to meet people while you do those things.

When I'm at the gym, I wear clothing with my company logo. I wear it when I go to the Lambo car meet-ups. I'm always networking, whether I am talking or sporting my brand because I never know who will need our services. When I'm talking to a guy and telling him what I do, and he says, "We need to have our roof looked at," —I've made a new contact and got a new contract.

Network with purpose and meet quality people that you will personally select to be in your life.

But make sure that you are actually networking when you network.

Some people play golf, for instance, but they are not there to meet people or improve their circle.

[
If you're networking with the same people all the time, you're not networking. You're just hanging out with friends.
]

If you're networking with the same people all the time, you're not networking. You're just hanging out with friends.

Also, when you're networking, you're not drinking. You're keeping your flow. You're expanding your circle at all times.

Here's another key: You're not going to be comfortable networking. The minute that you get comfortable, you've stopped networking because you've stopped reaching out to people. Networking is going to feel a little awkward.

Accept that it is awkward, and then do it anyway. But your mindset must be right there, directly influencing your networking in a positive fashion.

Networking should always be a natural part of your business and life! Practice these habits:

1. Build a Dream 25 List (These can be celebrities or people who you want to meet and become part of your network. Think big!!)

2. Meet at least three new people related to your business every day.

3. Take classes, join groups, embrace the hobbies and passions you love. Stop staying home. You won't meet anyone that way!

4. Make a list of the businesspeople in your area who you would like to meet.

5. Join mastermind groups with people who would love to do nothing more than push you toward your goals.

6. Note the people in your life who respond to your positive attitudes about things sarcastically, who don't ask about you, who don't call you, who don't make time for you, and who try to convince you to give up on your goals. Spend less time with them.

7. Eliminate narcissists, the one-uppers, the abusers, the toxic people who hurt you on purpose, or who claim their constant insults are a misunderstanding, that you "just can't take a joke." You have no time in your life for such people. Besides, you'll be too busy with your newfound friends who love the same things you do and who want more out of life.

I live what I am preaching every day.

Remember, you are working on creating positive habits. So, cut yourself a break if you fall off the wagon. Get right back on without beating yourself up, then re-center your focus because managing your life well and preparing to win means you cannot neglect the important Asset of Networking.

As you get started and try to find your footing, I'm going to be real with you. You will drop some of these six Asset balls, and that's okay! Just pick them back up and remind yourself that you are conditioning yourself to handle success and failure—as you perceive it in your eyes. However, you are less likely to drop any balls if you take care of these six areas every day.

When you concentrate on these Six Assets of Alignment, be assured that you are working in the right areas of your life. When you get used to changing where you exert your attention, you'll be better able to make lists that contain the actions you need to take for each area. Then you will have a better sense of how to move forward to live your best life and have it all.

MINDSET: THE CURE FOR WHAT AILS YOU

"Love challenges, be intrigued by mistakes,
enjoy effort, and keep on learning."
—Carol Dweck

This is the longest chapter because mindset controls everything in your life. There is a lot to cover, but hang in there, and please make sure to revisit this chapter when you need to.

SETTLING

We don't have a winning culture anymore.

That might not seem like a big deal, but lacking a winning attitude as a society can be incredibly detrimental to your own personal mindset and fatal to your motivation.

Everyone runs the bases, and they've stopped keeping score. I'm dreading the day when my daughters start playing organized sports because I suspect that they're going to stop keeping score. I know everyone is going to get a trophy—and I get that—but I worry about how I'm going to react to that. Of course, I want my daughters to feel like winners, but I also know they must learn HOW to win.

Lacking a winning attitude in society as a whole contributes to people settling and not trying as hard as they had to before. They feel that if they just go through the motions in their efforts that they will still get the award.

If you are not a top producer, ask yourself why. Do you think it has to do with the absence of a winning attitude in our society?

Take a look at the top two or three people earning more and winning more than you, month in and month out. What's different? Are they that much better than you? Or are they putting in the time that you're not?

Are you using the winning attitude in society as an excuse?

Are you *just good enough?*

Are you using the state of the market or the state of the world as an excuse?

Right now, everyone is griping about how the economy is slow because of COVID-19. And I get that. Depending on the state you currently reside in, there is some really strange stuff going on that may be limiting your resources and ability. (And if that's you—it's time to pivot, put your ladder on a different wall, and find an alternate path to success.) We're all essentially in the same boat here, but I'm not waiting for the phone to ring, even in the midst of a global pandemic. I am taking action to *make* the phone ring. I know that I can find a way to survive no matter what the platform is. My mindset is that solid, and—that is what sets me apart. It is what can set *you* apart, as well.

But anyone can piss and moan.

Anyone can pull back on spending when the rest of their industry does the same. I have multiple sales funnels. I run Google ads. I spend $20k a month on marketing because I know it's going to make $60k.

But I get where you are coming from if you aren't running with the ball. I haven't always been confident and proactive, as I've mentioned. I didn't have mentors telling me how to run my money.

I had to seek out coaches and mentors because no one around me understood what I wanted. No one could give me useful advice to help me progress.

I want to teach you how to operate in your world, in all aspects of your life, with an unflappable, indestructible belief in yourself—just the same as those people who believe and achieve.

So many people have said to me, "Burton, sure, I am probably settling, but my mind is at ease." Well, I don't believe it. Those kinds of people just have an overwhelming need for comfort and can't stand the tension of working hard.

The mindset of *just settling* occurs in all aspects of life. People settle in marrying somebody out of necessity because they gave up on their goals. Maybe they told themselves who they aren't, instead of who they really are.

After a few times of being kicked in the dating pool, the need for any kind of love, even love that isn't healthy, is good enough. They think subconsciously that if they just lower their standards, they won't be alone. When they meet someone who doesn't really 'light their fire,' they settle because at least they have someone to grow old with.

They get married to combine two incomes and have a decent life, and then they cycle through until they die—unfulfilled, weathering their existence. That mediocre reality isn't a way to live at all! People like this become expert justifiers and use platitudes like, "This is better than flying solo" and "You can't have it all." (Spoiler alert—I'm living proof that you can.)

People lie to themselves for decades until it's too late.

Settlers do such a fantastic job fooling themselves that they believe the crap they've programmed themselves to think. This subconscious habit is called *negative programming*, and it kills you a little bit every day.

What do you think? Are you guilty of doing this?

GO AFTER IT

I hope you will take away that anything you want is available and that you merely have to develop the fortitude to go get it.

[
Speak whatever it is that you seek into existence, and act as if you already have what you desire.
]

Speak whatever it is that you seek into existence, and act as if you already have what you desire.

It's absolutely crucial that you believe you DESERVE the blessings that will soon come your way, or else you may self-sabotage your newfound success.

I firmly believe that what you want is waiting for you. You just have to know how to ask for it, how to make it your own.

Knowing that what you want is out there is one thing. What's lacking is the knowledge of how to get it. *This* is why a lot of people give up so easily. *This* is why they get discouraged and lose sight of the blessings in their life. When this happens, folks stop moving toward their goals. In case you think I am talking in circles, gratitude and getting what you want and need from the universe are so deeply connected that they can't be separated. Do you believe me?

I read an article[1] that stated searching for gratitude is the same as finding it. That simple act, which takes mere seconds, starts to rewire your brain for the better ASAP. Gratitude also makes you more productive and allows you to address the elephant in the room: that productivity is possible through being positive.

Think about it. If you're ungrateful, sitting on the couch feeling sorry for yourself, how are you going to use negativity as the fuel to change yourself for the better? You can't. The two can never work together.

When you feel and show gratitude toward what you currently have, it doesn't give you an excuse to stop striving to reach new levels of success in all Six Assets. As you level up, your goals have to be adjusted, or you could backslide.

For example, maybe losing 20 pounds was a goal of yours, but then once you reached your goal weight, you cheated on your diet. You skipped a few workouts, and the next thing you know, six months has gone by. Not only did you regain the 20 pounds, but now you've added another five or ten pounds! You can never get too comfortable.

Meet your objective, and then move along to the next one.

Don't be the "someday" person. *Someday I'm going to retire. Someday I'll quit my job, etc.* When you do this, you're thinking so far in advance that you're not living in the now.

Ask yourself periodically: *What do I want now?*

Today has everything to do with your future. How you show up

at work and in the world proves what your future will be like.

Is what you are doing today more productive and better than yesterday? Are you still playing financial volleyball, or are you putting plans in place to work at that new idea that's been percolating in your mind for months? Are you holding yourself accountable to do something about it?

1   Clark, Carrie D. (2018). "How Gratitude Actually Changes Your Brain and Is Good for Business." Retrieved February 1, 2021, from https://thriveglobal.com/stories/how-gratitude-actually-changes-yourbrain-and-is-good-for-business/

If you are struggling with any of the above, a mentor can help you. As I move through my life and reset goals when I hit previous ones, I always have a mentor at my side. Mentors give you the non-biased opinions that you need to hear. They can unstick you out of *analysis paralysis* and keep you in check to ensure you are doing what you promised yourself.

And since our minds tend to get a little weak from the wrong conditioning, we have to use effective tools to keep them in top shape, so they can continue being productive.

Here are a few useful ideas for staying organized:

- Write down your goals daily.

- Get into a daily regimen that begins right when you wake up.

- Review your calls-to-action (CTA) or the steps you need to take to meet your daily goals.

- Identify and go after five big goals a year and reverse engineer the process you need to follow to achieve them.

- Be grateful and use daily affirmations to bring clarity to your mind.

- I am not a firm believer that your goals need to be super complex, but they do need to be written down so that your direction remains clear in your mind.

Let me also state that your goals should make you *uncomfortable*. Make them feasible, but at least somewhat hard to reach.

THE CARE AND FEEDING OF YOUR MINDSET

When I get up every day, my mindset is about winning the day. My thoughts go to what I need to do to get to the gym. I do my cardio before I go to work—two hours before I even start my business day.

I want to feed my mind the right fuel, too. There's something to the concept of preparing your mind to win. I don't flick on my phone and scroll Facebook. I grab an audiobook right away.

Just as we need to watch the fuel that goes into our body, we need to put our brains on a diet, too. My mental stimulation continues at the gym when I work out while listening to my book. So far, at that point in my day, I have done nothing but prep to win.

I don't want to live with the regret of not doing the right thing for me to be as healthy as I can be in all ways possible. If I want to have a good year, a good five years, or even a decade and beyond, I need to value waiting for the rewards I'm working for. I need to refuse to cave into instant gratification.

I encourage you to reprogram your mind, as well.

Wake up early.

Beat the late birds to the punch and increase your productivity by getting after it when everyone is sleeping.

Get up before sunrise, hop on a treadmill or Stairmaster, or take up yoga. Engaging in these types of exercises wakes you up—body *and* mind!

Training myself to hop out of bed and work out requires discipline. I don't put emotion into making the decision. It doesn't matter if I'm tired. I just take the action without second-guessing it. I feel good about working hard on myself when I realize I'm doing what other people aren't!

> **In addition to getting up and jump-starting the day, I ask myself, 'How many times can I win today?' It's a challenge that gives me a target to focus my attention on.**

In addition to getting up and jump-starting the day, I ask myself, How many times can I win today? It's a challenge that gives me a target to focus my attention on.

Another advantage? I can get out the door before any problems pop up. All of these thought processes contribute to the little game I play with myself of, *How much can I win today, and how far ahead can I get on potential issues?*

You want to have a winning mindset before an inevitable fire needs to be put out. That way, when the issues crop up—and it's life, so they will—you will be in the best mental shape to handle them.

THE EFFECTIVENESS OF DAILY AFFIRMATIONS

A number of years ago, I discovered that I needed daily affirmations. The biggest reason I started using them in my life was pretty simple and silly, really. I kept forgetting what I wanted to remember. I would get most of what I was trying to complete done, but it felt as if I wasn't doing enough.

A large part of why I think daily affirmations are so effective for me is that they remind me to be appreciative of where I am in each moment in my life.

Everything you write down won't necessarily lead to a new discovery, but, sometimes, when you actually sit down and write your daily affirmation, you are reaffirming what you already know.

As you learn about your daily affirmations, I want you to think about doing two things: taking account of where you are, and then asking yourself, *Where do I want to be?*

Do this, and you will know that you're achieving more and wanting more for yourself, your family, and, ultimately, your lineage down the road. What you do now is going to take care of your grandkids when you're gone.

Appreciate the *now*, as you honestly plan for tomorrow, and think about what allows you to stay humble.

I jot down that I'm grateful for my customers. I'm grateful for my loving family. I'm grateful for a home. I'm grateful that I can go to work.

I'm grateful that I have enough food to eat because there have been times where I've stolen quarters and scraped together pennies to have a meal. You don't forget that kind of thing, and I don't ever want to forget it. So don't let yourself get complacent.

Family and friends have pulled me aside and said, "Hey, man, you're pushing really hard." I hear them, but I won't be derailed from my intentions. It's human nature to want more. Your job—and mine—is to make sure that what you want cannot be construed negatively.

Start on your affirmations by getting vocal, even if you are only vocal with yourself, at first. The point is to get familiar with the power of your voice, to state, "This is what I need, and this is what I'm going after."

Your daily affirmations, of course, have everything to do with the Six Assets of Alignment. You want to affirm each of these areas of your life regularly.

Here are some examples you can practice on before you develop your own affirmations:

1. Mindset: I will defend myself against the demons in my life every day.

2. Faith: I will tell myself every day that life is working in my favor, as I refuse negative thoughts about my goals.

3. Family: I will make sure I tell the people I love the most that I love them once a day, at least.

4. Fitness: I will keep my commitment to work out once a day.

5. Finances: I will be open-minded to seeing financial opportunities.

6. Network: I will make connections with people who share the same hobbies and passions with me.

ORGANIZATION

I have the luxury of being self-employed, so I can determine when I start my day. When I wake up, I get all my personal items out of the way before my day begins. Then, when I am ready to start my business day, I can put my full attention on my job.

Because I compartmentalize my time well when I shift my time to my family, finances, or any other area of life, I can give each of them my full and undivided attention.

First thing in the morning, I write out my gratitude and my affirmations. I then spend 45 minutes listening to a book. Although I am not physically reading, *listening* is a productive way to consume a book. The trick is to multi-task. I listen to books while I am doing something else. Some days, I may listen at home while I am getting ready to go to the gym, and I will usually resume listening at the gym on the treadmill.

> *I've found that if I am listening to an audiobook while doing an activity like walking or running, it actually allows me to absorb the information better.*

I've found that if I am listening to an audiobook while doing an activity like walking or running, it actually allows me to absorb the information better.

When the brain is in beta mode—also known as normal functioning mode—there is too much external stimulation, and one is more easily distracted. So, my advice to you is to try to do two concentrated tasks at once, utilizing different senses, and experience and appreciate the difference in thought clarity and effectiveness.

KEEP YOUR PERSPECTIVE

Be honest about what you have accomplished and what remains to be done.

If I can't figure out how to move forward when I'm facing a dilemma, I might ask myself, *Is this person on this project in the right job?* or *Do I have the right people on board?*

Anytime I get stuck, I refer back to what needs to be done in the Six Assets, and that includes who is around me at that moment.

My vision is 100% my system. When I feel as if I am spinning my wheels, I know I can get out of the mental rut I am in when I dial into what the job is that needs tending to—whether that is a job I am responsible for or a job a team member needs to get after.

Taking this approach allows me to be non-emotional and pragmatic. You gain a clearer perspective on the truth of situations and what is needed to resolve challenges. You can operate on a higher level when you think this way. Even if you are not crazy about the next step or feeling a little weary from working, you will know what to do. You just have to make proper decisions and move forward.

TOOLS TO GET YOUR MIND RIGHT

Some people I have helped have told me that while they can pin down what they need to do, they don't know what to do first. This is why you must keep on top of what needs doing every day. Develop a solid and foolproof routine.

The more you practice the Six Assets, assessing what to do next and how to do it, the quicker you can figure out your next step and implement it. If you are not careful, it's easy to mentally masturbate all day long and *feel productive, but, in reality, not accomplish much.*

Give yourself five seconds to make a decision, like Mel Robbins insists: "Do not allow your brain to be involved [*with your decision*]. It all comes from your heart. If you wait longer than five seconds, you'll talk yourself out of making the decision."

The more you practice this, the nimbler your brain will become.

When it comes to improving your organization, organize what you want to throw away. Organize your clothes. Don't let useless things complicate your life. Take inventory mentally and physically. Simplify.

Your physical environment should be neat and clean, so you can think without distractions.

If you can't do it yourself, or you can't get started, hire somebody to keep your house in a state of less clutter. And when surfaces are clean, it allows you to clear the way for your inspiration. It is incredibly difficult to think properly in a dirty or cluttered environment.

I have people who mow the grass. And we don't even go to the grocery store anymore because our groceries are delivered.

What can you get rid of, and what can help you move more freely?

Consider it this way: One of your goals should be to earn enough income to free up your time for thinking and planning.

You groom your routine by starting new systems and keeping up with them. And we're not talking about the daily tasks and what has to be done. You're conditioning your mindset in this routine to follow through. This is one way your life can change.

Remember that as you are planning your life and carrying out your tasks to play to your strengths. I'm good at cleaning, but it's mentally taxing. Does it make more sense for me to have someone else clean so that I can spend that time setting appointments that are dollar-productive, or maybe I can gain more quality time with my family? You can't put a price tag on that!

FLATTEN FEAR

When you are afraid to take action, it helps to use the analogy of FEAR, "False Evidence Appearing Real." In laymen's terms, this phrase means that you can become so afraid of making a decision and so afraid of what you think the situation is going to be that you don't have a real appreciation for what needs to be done. Many times, what needs to be done is far less taxing than we believe. We usually don't have to go the extra mile that we have dreamed up in our heads.

Getting over your fear also means resisting self-sabotage. It's not about making a wrong decision. It's about taking a step forward, any step. It's about 'taking the swing,' not about how you swing the bat. Even if you take a wrong turn, remember you can use the Six Assets as a lifeline. Life might feel like it's falling apart, but you can cling to the foundation of the Six Assets.

Remember what Mel Robbins said: You've got to think—for five seconds—and then act. And don't forget that how you act will not always be perfect. That's okay. The point is to make progress. You can make small adjustments along the way to improve your performance.

There's the example of the guy who announced his goal to lose 20 pounds in one year. When I heard his announcement, I couldn't help but think, *You are definitely playing small! Why not 20 pounds in two months? Why are you not pushing yourself?*

I'm guessing he was afraid to make his goal too big.

Make your goals mean something. It can't be, "I need to make $1 million," when you are making $50k. Each goal should link to the prior goal. You might state that you will earn $100k, then $175, and then $250k, gradually stepping up your goals.

> *If you want to be a millionaire, ask yourself, Why do I want to be a millionaire? Then connect that goal to serving other people. Remember, abundance is tied to service."*

If you want to be a millionaire, ask yourself, *Why do I want to be a millionaire?* Then connect that goal with serving other people. Remember, abundance is tied to service.

ACTION STEPS TO REMEMBER

Before we move on, make sure you:

1. Set long-term goals.

2. Set short-term goals.

3. Allow yourself only five seconds to make a decision for daily challenges/problems that arise!

4. Take care of the Six Assets in your life.

5. Use mantras, repeated phrases, and famous sayings to remind yourself of what you want to do and how to do it.

6. Write out gratitude statements and remember the times when you wished you were where you are now.

7. Get organized.

Here's a little send-off for you as we end this chapter:

David Goggins wrote in his book, *Can't Hurt Me*, that he went through the Navy SEAL's BUD/S training three times. On his last try, David broke his legs from stress fractures brought on from the grueling training. But instead of quitting, he duct-taped his legs and finished. David lives by the mantra, "Be uncommon amongst uncommon people." That's the mindset we should strive for!

ALIGN YOUR EMPIRE

42

FAITH: LIFESAVING HOPE

"Feed your faith, and your fears will starve to death."

—Unknown

I am going to talk about religion in this chapter.

Does that surprise you?

To give you some context, I will share that I grew up Baptist—but I don't care about that, and neither should you.

Instead, let's focus on the importance of having something in your life that's bigger than you.

Faith can be bigger than religion.

I can hear your question already: *Why do I need to have something in my life that's bigger than me?*

Because you need to be tuned in to the universe around you. You need to know what blessings are in your life and be able to detect them when they arrive.

PRACTICING FAITH

Just because I am religious doesn't mean you have to be. And you can revere any higher power; you can meditate to get in touch with yourself and your thoughts. You can be spiritual and embrace what you don't *know*. There are many ways to speak to spirituality—as long as it works for you and helps you climb the right ladder against the right building. That's all that matters.

If you do have a higher-power view of the universe, doesn't it make sense that no entity above you would want you to suffer by rejecting your gifts? You are meant to be great and to discover your purpose to be happy. I can say this so emphatically because I have lived both ends of the spectrum—as the person denying himself everything because I didn't think I deserved anything good or anyone to love me, and as the person living out my highest desires.

Here's a rule I now live by: Don't let society or others with small thinking dictate or put labels on you. The more I reflect back over my life, the more I can see now that I was constantly bombarded by teachers, parents, and acquaintances about being "real" with my goals and dreams. And what they meant was that, based on my upbringing and how far behind the ball I'd started, I had to be realistic. I had to shoot well below the moon and try and fit in with my small-town upbringing.

These people who were trying to give me solid advice to save me from disappointment were trying to convince me that I was in the wrong to "think big."

But what they said never made sense to me. I knew in my soul that I was different. This is my gift, and I can finally recognize after many years that it's not a curse. I was angry for a time about my gifts. They felt too heavy to carry, and I blamed God for saddling me with them. I didn't have the faith that I could handle what He had given me.

FAITH IN OUR LIVES

Anytime anything successful has happened in my life, I knew I had help from a source outside myself. Every time I was at a fork in the road and trusted my intuition to guide me, I could sense a nudge to move in the right direction.

When you're in such situations, it's your mind's intuition that leads you, but there's also an external force guiding you along the way.

> *If you're putting out as much good as you can, it will come back to you, full circle. That's how the universe works.*

If you're putting out as much good as you can, it will come back to you, full circle. That's how the universe works. As long as you're placing yourself in the right situations, as long as you're helping other people and spreading as much positivity as possible, what you send out will come back to you.

The same is true of people with cynical minds. If you're out there doing shady business, guess what is going to come back and nip you in the butt?

Positive or negative, it eventually catches up with it you. Trust me—I have lived both of those realities.

In 2015, I was working in the health club industry. Since Ohio State University was right in my backyard and attracted all kinds of athletes and I was heavily into fitness, I was pegged as a guy who could help kids who were fighting themselves (and everyone around them) to get out of childhoods similar to mine. These kids' parents had signed them over to the state, so they lived in a group home where we could advocate for them since the parents had no say in their lives anymore.

Understand, the flow of good energy between the volunteers and the kids went both ways. Yes, I helped mentor these youngsters, but doing so was also healing for me. It was an honor for me to work with these children, who wanted to get out of circumstances they had been born into and had no control over.

Since I had escaped my upbringing and forged a new life for myself away from poverty, drugs, addiction, and abuse, the organization I worked with thought it would be great for kids to see that. These kids—who were mostly black—had endured poor interactions with white people, who they saw as oppressive and against them. I showed them differently. They thought it was pretty cool I had a sweet car and an IG account. I hoped it gave them goals to aspire to.

Over that year, I developed bonds with these young men. I like to think that they attached to me, too. I cared about them and their futures. I took up for them when their own parents couldn't be bothered. It meant the world to me that I was in charge of showing them that they could be cared for. Maybe I would be the one to finally impress that upon them. And I wasn't the only one who served in this capacity. NFL players and other sports figures were there for these little guys. We did everything we could to convince them they were worth having friendships with and being loved.

I got very close to one boy, Sean, in particular. He was trying his hardest to beat the forces holding him back. Sean had a lot of potential and played a mean game of football. When he was transferred to another school, the coach there told him he could play for their team. You can guess how thrilled he was. But in a twist that still makes tears come to my eyes, a screwup at the school held him back. One misstep literally robbed Sean of his chance to play. Some adult employed by the school or district to handle his records neglected to send his transcripts where they needed to go. It was a simple action that involved one step of follow-through, and it wasn't done. Even after the office uncovered the mistake, the people in charge said there wasn't anything they could do; without the transcripts, Sean couldn't play.

Sean talked to me about it and broke my heart when he said, "I just wanted to be a part of something."

This was a case of someone trying as hard as possible and using every tool they knew of to change their life—and other people failing him. On the ride home, after Sean tearfully confessed how hurt he was at this senseless neglect, I choked back my own tears so I could see the road ahead. I never let Sean see me cry, but I also never forgot that day.

I often think about the chain reactions of what we put out into the world. In the case of helping those kids, I envision that maybe down the road, they will remember their time with me. I can only hope they will use what they learned to make their lives better, to stop the negative cycle that they and their relatives (in many cases) have also lived. Maybe they will even go on to help someone else as they finally accept they can believe in the full power of themselves. As they finally grasp that they are worth it and have been all along—that's the highest proof of faith in ourselves.

BEING SPIRITUAL

I am not going to tell you that I go to church every Sunday because I don't. I also don't pray all the time, but I am strongly connected to the spiritual aspect of my life and participate in what I feel I need to do by giving back to others.

To me, the end-all and the be-all of spirituality involves karma, energy, and manifestation. It has everything to do with the intention that you push out into the world. Even if it doesn't sound like that's directly linked to faith, it is. When we answer what we need to do with our hearts, we have the faith it is going to work out and prove to be a good choice through the rewards we receive.

When you follow or utilize faith, you help yourself and others.

I have seen many people try to manifest what they want but then build a Plan B into their Plan A. When you do that, you are anticipating derailment. You are becoming a self-fulfilling prophecy and are destined to fail at your Plan A.

BE SPECIFIC WHEN YOU ASK

When I get very specific about what I want, God rewards me with what I asked for. It is with this concept in mind that I choose my opportunities.

I'm also a firm believer that we don't meet people by chance. When I communicate my intention, it then becomes my job to pay attention to what and who shows up in my life. It's my duty to see what is handed to me. When people enter my life, they are usually there for a purpose, and they usually have helped me meet my goals. You can fine-tune your self-awareness to be aware of such people in your own life, too.

THE SCARCITY MINDSET IS THE OPPOSITE OF FAITH

The scarcity mindset has everything to do with your relationship with the spiritual side of life. If you believe that you have to be careful about putting too much of yourself out there because you've received enough back, the universe will give—or not give, accordingly. The abundance mindset is one and the same with your spirituality, too. Speak it out, receive your gifts, and have faith that you will be taken care of. Give abundantly in your life, and you will receive abundantly. Hold on to every opportunity—even those that might not be yours (if you are the messenger and are supposed to pass on an opportunity)—and you will receive rewards.

When you're trying to swim upstream against your God-given talents, you're only helping yourself stay put.

SPIRITUAL REPRESSION AND REDEMPTION

My spirit was almost broken many times in my life. When I was only seven years old, I didn't have a good feeling about my situation. Life just didn't feel right. I wasn't happy. My parents were divorced, and my spirit was low. Other kids lived with their parents, but I was different. I started putting together what I thought my life could be like, and how I was living didn't match it at all.

We can think of such low times in our lives as spiritual repressions. This is when it's hard to have the belief that all will be well. Without the ability to think positively, you are definitely influencing your life. If you look at kids who grew up on the wrong side of the tracks, it makes sense that they sometimes never get out of their circumstances. Life eats them alive. The statistics of leaving poverty behind are incredibly slim.

This is why I am determined that my kids will grow up differently than me.

Go forward in faith, and you will receive rewards that will astound you.

GRAPPLING WITH RELIGION

At my fittest and when I was standing out in the competitions (as you will read about shortly), I was miserable. I felt I had lost my way in church, and the church did, too. It was crushing. All my self-hatred led to me almost losing my life.

What preceded my stay in the hospital came from allowing people in my head to sling their opinions at me. *I was a bad person. I was wrong. I was vain.* I heard it all. It made me suspect what I feared was true—*I truly was not a good person. I was shallow and didn't care about anyone else. A good person doesn't act that way.* I didn't want to be alive to hear about it anymore. And one day, I tried very hard to give myself a permanent time out.

I resented hearing what people had to say—the same secrets I held in my mind that they were saying out loud. It killed any potential to care about myself and turned deadly.

I let other people who were not happy with their own lives feed me their negativity. I didn't know my mission. I didn't know what I was supposed to be doing. This made me vulnerable to what people wanted to implant in my mind. Their negative attitudes and judgments manifested in me. The church, as I knew it at the time, hurt me especially. So many people who were a part of it: the pastor, my family, and friends had deserted me in my biggest time of need.

When I took in all their cheap shots, it almost took me out of the game.

My experience with my church prior to my overdose changed my faith. I am a much more spiritual person now, and I definitely respect a person's right to choose how they want to live their life despite their religion. It's not God or the actual belief system at fault in creating judgment. It's the people making up congregations that pervert religion.

But we do need faith. Pure faith. It's important, as I mentioned, to hold a belief in a power bigger than ourselves. And I actually think it empowers us.

If you are struggling with your faith and wanting to reconnect to your higher power, ask yourself: *How can I go forward in faith?*

If you are not struggling with your faith and are even proud of your devotion, I still want you to ask yourself, *How can I go forward in faith?* The reason is that we can always do more and show up in a more impactful and spiritual way.

My daughters have been baptized. This is a great path for our family as I work out and strengthen my own faith. I have a deep faith, and I allow myself to take the time to figure out if I want to be more religious or spiritual. I am happy to take the steps our family needs to take to be united in faith. You don't always need to know the answer. It is enough to get on the path and work on it as you go.

People distort religion and use it to their advantage. I can't begin to describe the level of betrayal this represents.

> *People distort religion and use it to their advantage. I can't begin to describe the level of betrayal this represents.*

Sometimes followers turn from the church and try to find their own truths. Wherever you are on your journey, it's okay.

I can say I was definitely turned off by the church following my experience in 2012, but I never turned from God. Daily, I am working to find my own truths with the help of the people who truly love me, and a heart rooted in faith. I trust that God let me stay here on earth for a reason.

For more help in getting clear on manifesting, refusing the scarcity mindset, and recognizing your God-given gifts, download my new Align Your Empire app to gain clarity in the Faith Asset. Just visit BurtonHughesOfficial.com.

FAMILY: LEANING ON AND LOVING THEM

"Everyone needs a house to live in,
but a supportive family is what builds a home."
—Anthony Liccione

My family is my rock, and I won't compromise when it comes to them.

I will always put them first.

I never want the people closest to me to doubt that I love them.

So I give them what they need in the form of action.

MAKING TIME FOR FAMILY

Every day, I *want* to spend time with my girls, and they *want* to spend time with me. It's not that every day is perfect, like a Disney movie (often streaming as background noise in our home). It's that I am putting in the work to get positive results. We all feel loved when we all choose each other every day. And at the end of each and every day, no matter how messy life may get—we are all still together, choosing each other, and in my opinion, that truly says it all.

I don't believe in showing up just 90% of the time—because you are either all in or all out! As a parent, I want to set the example of being a good father, one who my daughters can recall with warm feelings in their lives. I am building stability when I read to them and when I hear about their day or learn about their favorite things. I'm their dad, and I should know what kind of pizza they want. I love them, and when I don't know these little details, which are truly the big details in the grand scheme of things, it upsets me.

This is my standard and my value.

But it wasn't always this way…

SOMETHING IS MISSING

When I was younger and working in new home sales, I was making decent money. I had a big house I rattled around in all by myself. I was honing my physique and working on my health.

But something was still missing.

I couldn't put my finger on it.

It was the end of June when my brother Dan called me and said, "I need your help." I didn't know what he needed, but that didn't matter. I was all-in, immediately. Even though we're brothers, we don't call each other often. So, when the phone rang in the middle of the afternoon, and I saw his name pop up on the screen, I knew something was wrong.

Dan said he was in a jam. He needed to move back home, but he wasn't moving in with Mom.

In my ultimate bachelor pad, I could walk around in my underwear any time I wanted and never worry about a thing. But my brother needed help, and I would do whatever I could to be there for him.

But it wasn't just my brother who would be crashing at my house. That following weekend when Dan moved in, he brought with him three young daughters, his wife, and their two dogs. Needless to say, my house was a bachelor pad no more! I didn't hesitate to welcome Dan and his family into my home because it was the right thing to do, and he would have done the same for me.

This was one of those enlightening times we experience throughout life. God really does have a funny way of putting you in situations to teach you exactly what you need to learn. Because within a mere few days of Dan's family moving into my place, I realized what I was missing. My eyes were suddenly opened.

I watched Dan's daughters come down the stairs every morning, racing over to him and squealing, "Daddy! Daddy!" before leaping into his arms.

It was beautiful. I couldn't believe how lucky he was.

I was making good money. I had a nice house. I had the physique. But it was all so superficial. It didn't mean anything. I was pushing so hard in these areas of my life, but I was neglecting the opportunity to build a family and share my life with them.

Dan and his family showed me that I was missing out on something so much greater—something that could only enhance the areas of my life I had been working so hard on.

Up until this point, all I knew was that I didn't want to be like my parents, so I ran from any sort of commitment.

I never wanted to get married. I never wanted to have kids.

I thought if I had kids, I would have to give up on my dreams. What I didn't know yet was that I had a scarcity mindset—because I'd watched my parents and the way they handled parenting.

They were busy. They were angry. They took it out on their kids. I didn't want that for my family. And I started to realize it didn't necessarily have to be that way.

> *But I wasn't my parents. I was in control. I could break the cycle.*

But I wasn't my parents. I was in control. I could break the cycle.

Many times, when people get married, they see it as the end goal. They give up and stop trying. They aren't romantic. They forget to put their spouses first, and when that happens, love decays.

When you start having kids, you need to take stock of what you envision for your family and what you want your life to be like.

My childhood cemented in my head what I *don't* want for my girls. From feeling the pain of missing out, struggling, and navigating the world largely alone as a kid, I knew I didn't desire that for my children. I want them to be able to call on their strong family for support when they need it, and not just when they're at a crossroads, but every day, no matter how petty things might seem.

> *My little, precious family has been a way for me to rewrite my history. It's given me an ending to my childhood story. Through a healthy family life, I have broken the cycle. This reinvention makes me a better man, all the way around.*

My little, precious family has been a way for me to rewrite my history. It's given me an ending to my childhood story. Through a healthy family life, I have broken the cycle. This reinvention makes me a better man, all the way around.

I'm happier, and this comes from choosing to love the people in my life wholeheartedly every day.

TEACHING THROUGH LOVE

I know that being with my daughters and reinforcing positive images of themselves helps prevent eating disorders. I know that honoring and respecting their mother will show them the type of relationships they deserve. My actions give them so many resources to attain mental wellness. They are less likely to have drug and alcohol issues, and they are more likely to achieve academic goals.

It may not be easy, but I'm certain your family is worth it. You made a commitment to the people closest to you. Don't take that commitment lightly.

TEACHING THROUGH LOVE

Mental toughness allows you to fight for what you want in your relationships, and more importantly, to keep it.

Let me assure you that every marriage will have its problems. The solution is to solve them immediately, so they don't fester and grow to become something you can no longer deal with. Don't lie to each other. Be truthful, yet fair, when you fight. Have the tough discussions together. Keep the lines of communication open at all times. Then if you get into a real bind, you will know that resources are available.

Show respect for your marriage and stay away from situations that aren't good for your union. Try to mitigate any type of risks that might lead to misunderstandings or hurt feelings.

Your spouse doesn't need to have unnecessary worries. When you commit to protecting them, you save your partner pain because they will know your conduct is always on the up and up.

The foundation of family is love and respect. That foundation stays solid when you show people through your actions that they matter. You don't need to complicate your relationships. I have learned that people want to be chosen and shown they are cared for. Period.

ALL IN AND ALL OUT

Shortly after Dan's family joined me, I shifted from working in real estate and got into turning around underperforming health clubs. It turns out I'm pretty decent at selling personal training and resuscitating gyms.

Think of the show *Bar Rescue*, but imagine doing the same thing for health clubs in Central Ohio and South Florida. That's what I was doing. I was good at it and enjoyed the work.

I would go into health clubs as a "secret shopper" with a three-day pass to work out. The whole setup was pretty simple.

As I worked out over the three-day period, I observed the state of the club. I watched the front desk. I watched the janitor. I watched the spin classes (but I steered clear of the yoga classes—because flexibility is not my thing!).

[
Think of the show Bar Rescue but imagine doing the same thing for health clubs in Central Ohio and South Florida.
]

I had a great time doing these rescues. I met a lot of really cool people and learned a lot about myself. But I still wasn't sharing my life with someone—so there was a definite void.

Although I was dating, I was failing relationships left and right. Despite my achievements in a few areas of my life, I was depressed.

I was experiencing success on stage at competitions and even won the Mr. Ohio Bodybuilding Championship. But my path wasn't right, and I could feel it.

I took some time off from competing. I wasn't happy with where I was spending my time, and I wasn't soundly confident with what I wanted to accomplish.

As all of this was going on, Ashley, my girlfriend, and I got married. But our relationship was strained, at best.

She and I had known each other since childhood. She was safe and felt like home, but I was lost. While I tried to pursue a new career in fitness, I simultaneously watched my marriage fall apart, almost in slow motion.

In the fall of 2011, I returned to the national competition stage. I was qualified to compete at Nationals after winning the Mr. Ohio title in my weight class the previous year.

I trained very hard that year, and after busting my butt and sacrificing, I won the Men's Physique class, which, by definition, made me one of the top IFBB (International Federation of Body Builders) Pro Men's Physique competitors in the world.

Now, I don't want you to think that I looked like, or that I am, the size of Arnold Schwarzenegger. This Physique class was geared more toward a health and wellness/aesthetic look. Think Matthew McConaughey in board shorts for a visual.

Although I had won such a high award, I felt hollow because I had shut out everything and everybody. I wasn't overly egotistical, but bodybuilding is a singular sport, and that singularity ruins relationships.

I'd put my performance first, before finances and any meaningful relationship, including my marriage. While becoming successful in the realm of fitness, other areas of my life had eroded, and I'd simply watched and let it happen. It was like an out-of-body experience.

I had hit pro status and really thought I had 'made it.' I felt like a superstar; my social media platforms were going gangbusters, and my DMs were blowing up—I was the 'Big Man on Campus'—but the campus wasn't real. The reality was that I still had to go back to work on Monday. Despite my success on stage and in the fitness world, I was in the wrong place in my life. That led to feeling unfulfilled with an overall negative attitude.

Being unable to turn off my passion for working out and the clubs I was helping to turn around, as well as not knowing how to manage my depression, doomed my marriage. This is not to say I was the only one at fault. In every relationship, both people must contribute, but I didn't make it easy on us.

Not surprisingly, Ashley left me. Our circumstances weren't helped by my jumping into the world of fitness with both feet and becoming a full-time fitness model. But I don't regret doing it, either.

During the time I was pursuing this new exciting chapter in my life, Ashley and I had been trying to start a family. After three miscarriages, the doctors couldn't explain why we'd lost the babies. I dealt with our loss in a cold, dismissive manner and tried to be the tough guy. I would say, "Everything happens for a reason," but, in reality, I was having a hard time with it. My wife could no longer stand the person I had become. She left me in South Florida and returned home to Ohio. I couldn't blame her, as most people didn't want to be around me, either. I didn't want to be around me. I did try to save the marriage, but it was too late.

I was about to enter the darkest days of my life.

It's not surprising that I was hit so hard by depression. I was losing myself and the dreams of my family. I didn't know about the Six Assets of Alignment yet, and so every one of the wheels on my car was pointing in the wrong direction.

I hadn't prioritized my relationship and had chosen to run from my problems. What did I think was going to happen?

Relationships and marriages are supposed to last forever, but sometimes, they don't. Still, we need to forgive ourselves if that happens. We have to choose our family, love them, and keep our promises to them. But we can never lose sight of living our lives with pride in alignment. Remember, the goal isn't to score an A+ in the Six Assets of Alignment. It is to learn in each of these areas what you need and to make sure that you are true to yourself.

Do that, and you will feel secure enough to take care of everything else, no matter what comes up. No matter the changes that might hit you that you have no control over.

The Six Assets of Alignment is your lifeline that will keep you steady in relationship changes.

When you take care of the Family Asset, it will ensure you are the happiest in all your relationships because you will be getting what you need as you love the people around you.

Happy people go after what makes them joyful, and then they spread that joy to their family and the people closest to them.

FITNESS: PURSUING IDEAL HEALTH

**"Work out because you love your body,
not because you hate it."**
—Unknown

I go to the gym every morning and afternoon for 45 minutes.

Maybe that seems excessive, but it works for me and allows me to look and feel the way I want.

That's the theme of this chapter: finding what works for you in pursuing ideal health. Honestly, that is the goal of every aspect of fitness.

I don't want you to blindly subscribe to any fitness or nutrition regimen. Just make it a point to practice maintaining your fitness and eat as well as you can.

You don't need to be talked down to or told what to do. You can figure out what your body is asking for. Listen to your body. Seriously, it *will* tell you what it needs.

I'm sure you've thought about your physical health a lot and about what is lacking. Most people who are not on top of their health spend time worrying over it.

If that's you, not to worry. This is the time to step up and take ownership of your fitness—whatever that means for you.

SUBCONSCIOUS FITNESS

I am now on autopilot when it comes to my fitness. I don't think about what I should do or need to do. I am proactive in staying fit and healthy. It's another non-negotiable in my life. Every day, I give myself the gift of two workouts and make no excuses.

Maintaining your fitness and physique is far easier than getting into shape—and when you are on the diet-and-fitness roller coaster with thousands of stop-n-go's, it's a pain to work toward your fitness goals over and over again. Not to mention, it's really hard on your body!

This is why I never let myself get out of shape or overweight. What a grueling journey back to health that would be! I don't want to work that hard when I don't have to. All I need to do to stay on track is think about the time when I was 50 pounds overweight and couldn't climb the damn stairs!

Every meal I eat contains foods that fuel my body and my mind! The better you feel, the better you will perform in your career and everything else in between. Now, let's be clear, I'm not saying that you cannot indulge every now and again, but it needs to be in moderation and maybe as a reward for the past week's effort. Be careful when you do allow yourself a little treat because this is when we are most apt to fall headfirst off our health wagon!

[
*I want to be the role model for how people can look their best,
and I don't want to have regrets about neglecting my body.*
]

My body is also one of my sources of income, and, admittedly, that makes it easier for me to be more disciplined. If I want to cash the checks, I need to do the work. And as you know by now, in this book, the work you do predicts your results. *I'm not interested in the results I don't want, so I stay ready.*

I want to be the role model for how people can look their best, and I don't want to have regrets about neglecting my body.

You and I both know these efforts go far beyond what you see on the surface.

And like everyone else, I wish there was an easy button to push, but fitness is a continual mental and physical conditioning process.

NOT LIVING TO YOUR FULL POTENTIAL HURTS—AND CAN KILL YOU

When I didn't live up to my full potential, it almost ended me —

And that's how critical it is to make sure your Assets of Alignment match your values.

At the darkest period of my life, I couldn't see anything that was important anymore. I was just going through the motions with no idea of what the actions I was taking meant, or didn't mean, for that matter.

After securing a few weeks of my *head pills* (as I liked to refer to them), I went back to my old church to join a prayer group in an effort to better myself and my life. At the men's Wednesday night discipleship, I told the group, "Look, I just need to find my center, to become whole again."

But when I shared what I was going through, I didn't feel welcomed or encouraged—instead, the church judged me.

> **But when I shared what I was going through, I didn't feel welcomed or encouraged—instead, the church judged me.**

By then, I was modeling and had been on the covers of hundreds of romance novels. I'd been cast in reality TV shows and was on the covers of various magazines. I'd even shot a campaign for a swimwear company based in Australia that would get me exposure on the other side of the world. This was frowned upon in the church's eyes.

"You're going against God," they told me. "It's no wonder you're getting divorced." "How could you have a family? Look at you! You're all over the Internet. What's the matter with you? This is not how you're supposed to live, Burton!"

My life was thrown back into a loop.

Church was where I'd intended to turn my life around. Instead, they made me feel unwelcomed. That feedback got the best of me, and I relied on the pills to numb me, to turn off the pain. It was easier than feeling emotions—until it wasn't.

I was about to discover that I couldn't keep running from life. I could ignore my needs for a while, but the ghosts that haunted me would keep returning.

On the morning of September 16, 2012, I was sitting in my car before work. I wasn't even having a bad day. It wasn't yet 9:00 AM. My hand clutched that bottle of anti-anxiety pills. And then—I ate them all, every last pill in that bottle.

When you are empty inside, it's easy to collapse and die.

I nearly did that day, sitting in my car in the parking lot—after setting my life on a downward trajectory.

After not seeing my value.

After denying help.

I almost lost it all, and by the time I came out on the other side, I'd made a doctor's head spin.

"You're very lucky," he told me. "Most people don't survive what you did."

I had set myself up in all the wrong ways in every area of my life, and I was about to pay dearly.

Writing about this time of my life is difficult for me. It's hard to get down on paper. Not necessarily because of the vulnerability it took to share my attempted suicide, but because I needed to ensure I shared the *right* details that led up to this point with you. I obviously introduced you to my childhood in previous chapters, but there were specific experiences as a young man preceding my overdose that I deem pivotal in understanding my personal awakening—which occurred at the darkest stage of my life.

But by the Grace of God, I'm here today to share with you how I managed to reorganize my mind and life, setting me forth on the path that I now know I am destined for. *The path that brings you and me together. Here. Now.*

THE END OF ME ... ALMOST

In only a few moments, my body had 29 Ativan floating around inside it.

Eight can kill you, by the way.

If they don't kill you, you're typically destined to live like a vegetable for the rest of your life.

After I took those 29 Ativan, I walked into work and blacked out.

When I woke up in the hospital, the nurses told me in between temp checks and IV pokes, "You have more people coming through those doors than any other patient we've seen" As one nurse reached behind my head to adjust the pillow, she said with a smile, "You must be something special!" All I could do was smile back as I tried not to cry.

I had overdosed, but I wasn't an alcoholic or a drug addict.

If you had been an outsider looking in, you would have seen a sad soul trying to fill an empty void. I was quick to put my newfound 'fame and popularity' in front of everything. Maybe it was my drive and ego that ultimately got the best of me. I know my life looked miserable to the people around me. I know I looked lost. I was. I was being torn in two directions. I don't know if I was dealing with a fight between my head and heart or between internal and external forces, but damn! I was all messed up.

I had strayed too far from who I was. I was trying to be someone I wasn't. Being a professional fitness model was *what* I did. It wasn't *who* I was. Once I acknowledged and embraced that slight difference in my approach to life, I could get my arms around how I could leverage my success and use it for good—but it wasn't a quick fix or an easy road, and, first, I was going to have to survive what I'd done in that car.

I had lost any self-awareness I'd had. Without that, hard times lay ahead, I promise. There's no control. There is only depression and anxiety—and darkness. Everything moves fast, but in slow motion. Looking back, as I sat in the parking lot, bottle of pills in hand, I was fighting to salvage something, anything in my life. Nothing was working. Too many things were too late. I looked around and felt that I had set fire to everything and everyone around me.

I was fighting with myself, with the people I'd lost, and with the will to live. I didn't know whether I could get out alive. I didn't want to be a statistic, but I didn't have the tools I needed to dig myself out of such a deep emotional hole.

On the day I swallowed that bottle of pills, I'd had enough of feeling indifferent. I just wanted the pain to stop. I knew they would do the job. They should have done the job. But one thing is certain – a higher power had different plans.

So, while I will never condone taking a month's worth of anti-anxiety medication, it taught me that I was not forgettable. And that changed the trajectory of my life. It was something I needed to know.

REDEEMING MYSELF

Once I was out of the hospital and recovered, I was embarrassed at what I had done. But if I was going to claw my way up to having a worthwhile existence, I had to suck it up. I would no longer let anyone or anything—not even myself—stop me. I wanted more for myself and knew something bigger was out there. The more that I considered the odds I'd beaten, the more convinced I became that *I was meant to live.* At such a young age, with no adult wisdom, I fought as hard as my body and mind would allow. My fighting to survive hadn't let up—even into adulthood. No wonder I was beyond exhausted, wasted.

Deep down, I didn't want to die. I'd never wanted to die—not even when I was that abused little boy, but certainly not after my suicide attempt.

When I realized that, everything began to change.

I could accept what I had lost because I knew what was to come.

As soon as I was released from the hospital, I set out to reinvent myself and become a better person, to live with fulfillment and gratitude. I had work to do, but I knew I could and would do it.

After the doctor explained how lucky I was, the thought circled in my brain for a while: *What a close call! Why did I live? I am so lucky. I don't want to die. But why was I spared?*

Had I suffered a brain injury, it would have been a fate worse than death.

After I got over the shock of learning what could have happened, I figured that I couldn't go back to the way things had been. I had to accept that Ashley had left. I had to move on and stop fighting for the relationship that was no longer meant for me.

To think of what the future could be as I was recovering—was overwhelming at times, but it was also a gift. Add that to the fact that I learned people cared about me, and it made me extremely emotional.

Healing from the attempted suicide didn't happen overnight. My brain was spread all over the place, and there was no order to any of my thoughts. I had a mind full of surviving, healing, and longing. How could I understand what needed to be changed so that level of misery would never happen again?

I knew it would require a ton of concentrated work, but I had no doubt that I could and would do it.

THE AFTERMATH

Following my overdose, doctors confirmed there was really nothing wrong with me. I didn't have ADHD. I didn't even have a condition that warranted the anxiety prescription. I should never have been told, "Take this pill, and it will fix your anxiety."

Instead, I just wasn't living up to my full potential. Now, I am resolved that I will never let anyone else tell me what's good for me and what I need to do.

Naturally, fitness spills over into improving your mindset. It helps my moods stay on an even keel when I work out. I express frustrations and pent-up energy as I increase testosterone and motivation.

There are so many undeniable benefits that it's easier for me to commit to taking care of myself when I keep them in mind.

I hired a coach, a trainer, and a dietician when I wanted to ramp up my fitness to a better level. I then used their energy and redirected it into making sure I was doing my workout. I made sure that I was following my cardio programs, fulfilling my sleep needs, and sticking to my nutrition plan. I needed a mentor to lead me into being the best version of myself. (It's always okay to ask for help. In fact, the self-awareness it takes to realize you might *need* a little outside influence truly should be commended.)

I am saving time knowing what to do, and I'm able to operate at a different level because I'm not just winging everything. I can't imagine how people can get anything done without a plan. I must have a routine that I follow almost religiously. This is why I teach my clients how to follow a similar regimen that works for them. And why I recommend the same regimen for *you*!

You'll also find that when you live up to your full potential and stay in control in one area, it leads you to gain control in others. Suddenly, you'll use your surges of energy much more productively.

EXTREME AND INSPIRING CONTROL

One of my clients taught me what an extreme grip on control looks like:

She told me, "I got bad news. I went to the doctor, and they told me that I have high blood pressure and cholesterol. I'm on the verge of diabetes."

I reassured her that we would figure it out, no matter what had to be done.

She went on, "My doctor told me to lose 100 pounds."

Well, I was right on top of that! We set up a phone call to develop a plan since she lived up in the New England area. "We've got 12 months," I told her, hoping that devising a strategy would remove the panic.

"This is your meal plan. We are going to focus on getting you to lose 1.92 pounds a week, not 100 pounds because if you think of it that way, you're lost. You're done." She agreed and was eager to get started!

This gal followed our plan to the letter. Her ego wasn't in the way. She was coachable. (Let me remind you that she was in her late forties.) Ten months later, she went to her follow-up appointment with the doctor, and they didn't recognize her.

She'd lost 110 pounds in 10 months and she sent me a photo of her standing in one of her pant legs. She was no longer pre-diabetic, and she didn't have high blood pressure. She stopped her cholesterol medicine and was healthy.

During that same time, she received two job promotions. As she refused to settle with her health, she adopted the same attitude in other areas of her life. She got better. Her relationship with her kids and her family improved, too.

You know why?

Because money doesn't buy confidence. My client needed to take ownership of the physical fitness in her life, and she did.

We all need to feel that we have control, especially if we're Type A people. If you don't have that base level of organization to gain that control, you're done. You won't reach any goals. Not only that, but it will drive you crazy!

TYPE A PEOPLE AND ADDICTS—SAME THING?

Type A people are obsessive, and sometimes they are that way because they have an addictive personality.

Most addictive people bounce around. Their addictive personality sets them on one path, and then they get all juiced up and move onto another path. I have also found that people with these addictive personalities will go all in on whatever they are doing. It might be gambling for a few months, for instance, before they turn to punishing themselves at the gym.

If you do this, you're simply substituting one addiction for the next. That's how you crash and burn.

You'll drive yourself into the ground and then have to reinvent yourself again. Are you going on all cylinders at work while you are afraid of coming home and being intimate with your partner?

That's just one manifestation of addiction and how we can use this trait to avoid and enlarge the problems in our lives.

Let's get to the bottom of what your addictive cycle may be.

To determine this, look back at your history. Do you typically take something on and then attack it until you lose interest? Are you then forced to reinvent yourself? When this was me, I wanted to know why I was acting this way. If this is you, why wouldn't you want to know the same?

Do you justify what you want to do, even if it means your work will suffer?

Do you immerse yourself in other forms of addiction to self-sabotage your success?

Are you addicted to the result?

What kind of people are you spending time with?

> *Who you are attracts the type of people you have in your life. If you are a schmoozer, boozer, cheater, job hopper, afraid of intimacy, etc., then you will want people around you who live those ideals—because we want to surround ourselves with people we can relate to.*

Who you are attracts the type of people you have in your life. If you are a schmoozer, boozer, cheater, job hopper, afraid of intimacy, etc., then you will want people around you who live those ideals—because we want to surround ourselves with people we can relate to.

And we certainly seek out people who think like us in the area of fitness because working on your health is hard work, and requires numerous and consistent sacrifices.

JUSTIFYING EXCUSES

If you're reading this and thinking, *I've got a dad bod or a mom bod, and I'm fine*, that's okay. So long as you're *truly* okay with it, great! If deep down, you're not, then define your goal and kick yourself in the ass. Or better yet, drive yourself to the gym.

If you need another reason to head to the gym, you should know that you will feel sharper after a workout, and that will happen on a regular basis when you are constantly maintaining a healthy body.

The better shape you're in, the more open your neurological pathways will be. People who are healthier and more physically active are smarter and learn things quicker.

Let's not kid ourselves. When you feel and look your best, you're going to perform better across all Six Assets. Start now! Make your fitness and nutrition plan today.

FINANCES: MAXIMIZE YOUR LIFE BY CHANGE (AND DOLLARS)

"Beware of little expenses.
A small leak will sink a great ship."
—Benjamin Franklin

Your winning finance formula:

1. Pay your bills.

2. Make more money if you need it to pay your bills via side jobs, part-time gigs, etc.

3. The focus should be on earning and generating more income! Most people are so caught up in saving money that they don't think of areas where they can earn more! Get on offense!

I've found that there's magic in the number three. That's one of the reasons I like the 1, 2, 3 formula above.

And you can count three things on one hand and remember them.

Plus, I don't want to make this complicated because managing your money doesn't have to be complex.

First and foremost, you've got to take care of your bills.

If you are in a job that is making paying your bills difficult, I encourage you to find a way to fix that. Pronto.

The only true measuring stick in business is the answer to this question: *How much new business are you closing?* The second question that holds any weight is, *How are your finances going to affect your family?* Knowing that most relationships fail due to money was a huge motivator for me to get my money situation right.

NO MORE MISTRUTHS

Before we go any further, I want to take a minute and set straight a few untruths. You may have heard people say, "Money doesn't make you happy." I'll put it to you this way: If someone gave you a million dollars right now, what would you do with it? What problems would it solve for you? Could you pay off your student loans? Could you get rid of medical bills? If you did that, how would your life change? How much stress would instantly be lifted off your shoulders?

Granted, if you're an unhappy degenerate, you might have a harder time believing that money might help. Maybe you are determined to be miserable no matter what. I can't help you with that—you need an attitude adjustment.

When I didn't have enough money in my life, my stress was the highest it had ever been.

Becoming successful introduces new options into your life. You can make moves to resolve problems that have plagued you for a long time. You can stop worrying about how you will take care of your family.

There were times in my life when I didn't have enough cash. I had to scrape enough together to put gas in my car, so I could get to work. Who wants to live like that? It gets old very fast, and it is exhausting. It is especially exhausting if you have to do it over and over again, or if you have to pull from reserves that are quickly drying up. The same can be said if you have to reinvent yourself every day to resuscitate hope. Wouldn't it be nice to take a break from constantly searching for ways to simply survive?

SUCCESS IN YOUR GOALS

So many people don't know what their short-term and long-term goals are. You need to know them to make sure your day-to-day needs are being met. Take care of your bills, mortgage, utilities, and business expenses that keep your doors open. Once you've handled the smaller daily goals, then you can focus on more long-term goals, like what investments you want to make.

You want to know that you can retire. No one wants to pinch pennies and drastically change the quality of their lifestyle by reducing their output when they are old and gray. Yet, people do this to themselves when they don't plan properly. When you're 50 years old and hoping that you can swing the house payment in 10-15 years, that's not a plan. Being a greeter at a department store is not a plan. Inaction in favor of desperation when you will be tired and maybe even unhealthier is not a plan.

[***Don't you think you owe yourself an easier life?***]

Don't you think you owe yourself an easier life?

All it takes is a little planning and discipline. It's better to have the discipline now when the stakes aren't quite so high and when you have more of an ability to make money if you get in a bind.

If you're successful, you're going to feel good. If you have money in your pocket as a result of being successful, your mindset will transcend the worries that you would face otherwise. If all your credit cards are maxed out, and you're on the verge of bankruptcy, how do you think you will feel? If you had the option to not feel that way, wouldn't you take it?

MONEY FOLLOWS PASSION AND APTITUDE

In my financial life, I had to find the right vehicle and career path. I had to get my assets back into alignment and attach to a purpose that was about more than making money.

What I needed and wanted to do had to physically and financially pay off. I knew if I was doing what I loved, I would be successful.

My main source of money was real estate. I was confident it would pay off for me because the major earners in America and the people with excessive money all dabble in sales and real estate. I enjoy both, so it was a logical choice.

It really does work out best for everyone if you tap into your God-given talent. Sure, we can talk about all the logistical steps you need to take, such as paying off your credit cards and car, for instance. We obviously know that we want to get rid of any bankruptcies on our credit reports. That's all common sense.

The bigger picture is how to combine your financial goals with the right financial and business vehicle. You need to know what you are good at (and please don't take offense when I state that no one is good at everything).

It's true.

> *I would rather be exceptional in a select few specialties than mediocre in all areas.*

I would rather be exceptional in a select few specialties than mediocre in all areas.

When I ask young people, "What do you want to do?" they might say they should be a doctor because doctors make a lot of money.

My next question to them is, "But is that what you *want* to do?" *That's* where we should start when we decide our business of choice—learning what we *want* to do. We can build the business offerings from there.

Your career and what you love to do should also generate *real* money that you can make a *real* living from.

I'm specifying what I mean, here, with emphasis since so many people equate the work that needs to be done with what they see on Instagram—the fake profiles that show people posing as influencers. Such people give you the wrong idea of what you need to do to create lasting wealth. People like that only show you what they want you to see. You don't know the truth of their lives, so don't base your money on that.

Figure out how to love what you do while you get paid for it.

GENERATE SOLUTIONS, NOT JUSTIFICATIONS TO PLAY SMALL

Just like what we see on social media may not be true, you don't want to spend money just to look cool. Always live within your means.

> *Here's a secret: People who have real wealth are not interested in posing. They don't care if they look rich or not. They're too busy working to peacock around, pretending to have stuff they don't.*

Here's a secret: People who have real wealth are not interested in posing. They don't care if they look rich or not. They're too busy working to peacock around, pretending to have stuff they don't.

When I got divorced, I had to file for bankruptcy. It sucked, but it also showed me what I was made of. As soon as I filed, I hit my work as hard as I could to try and put it behind me as quickly as possible.

If you are in a similar situation, there is no need to remind yourself of how far behind you feel you are all the time. Just focus on your goals. How many more deals a day can you close? Before you hang it up for the night, can you make one more call? What can you do in five minutes? Did you work 40 hours or only four because you were on your phone?

I still work in a similar fashion as when I held my two part-time jobs, and my productivity continues to be enviable. When I increased my productivity, it increased my income so I could do more long-term investing.

I advocate handling your financial matters in this way because cutting back doesn't work. Most people want to live a certain lifestyle. They get used to creature comforts, and it is exceedingly difficult to remove those versus adding them—meaning, if you are in a tough spot, instead of slashing the budget, get to work! There are all kinds of opportunities out there to make additional money. If you can't find any, you aren't looking hard enough!

You might think this sounds weird, but I like being a little uncomfortable. In fact, I really don't want to be comfortable. I work toward being at least slightly uncomfortable at all times, and that means pushing myself to make as much income as possible. Pushing myself makes me feel human. It makes me appreciate how good I really do have it. It keeps me hungry, and when I know I need to put it all out there to make more and prove more to myself, I will.

I recently had a conversation with a gentleman about selling his house and downsizing to a small apartment for $1,400/mo. I asked him: "Do you want to leave where you are now?" Well, of course, he didn't want to. He liked his place. He simply wanted to be more comfortable.

He was essentially talking about minimizing everything and figuratively eating bologna sandwiches. He is also married, and so I questioned if his wife was on board with these lifestyle changes.

He had never even asked her opinion! I came at him with a different response than I imagine he ever expected. I told him I thought making these major lifestyle changes while in his thirties might be counter-productive for his future. Needing less might lead to doing less and ultimately lower his goals in accordance with his newfound threshold.

I believe having a little debt puts a fire in people's bellies to work harder and strive for more success. If this guy followed through on his plan, he would be swinging the pendulum too far backward—it would be extremely hard to get back to what he is earning now. He might also find that without meaning to, he lowers his standards.

YOUR BRAIN WILL TRICK YOU

No matter your financial situation, your brain will trick you. Since our brains are there to protect our bodies, they will assess your risk and try to mediate it. If you are worried about making money, your brain will compel you to earn more. If you are leading a life where money isn't stressful for you, then it follows that you would not want to work too hard. Your brain would do its best to tell you, "You don't need to do much here. Go ahead and relax."

We also know that your brain will push you to perform according to what other people are doing. When you think about it, why would you want to do something that no one else wants to do? You will assess what is going on around you and try and be a part of it—even if it means you won't earn your potential.

This is why it can be a little awkward to go against the grain. I felt that way momentarily when I doubled down on my business this year. But that sensation only lasted a minute because my success came crashing through.

A little bit of discomfort leads to more feelings of self-empowerment—especially when you come up with a new business model or resolve a financial pickle using fresh innovation that you cooked up. That's when you learn you truly are invincible, that you have held the power all along, that you are brilliant and not just when your back is against the wall, but always—as long as you have the confidence to find new ways to succeed.

So don't be afraid to push yourself and get a little uncomfortable. Stay hungry, but don't starve yourself, and use the money you do make to invest in your long-term goals.

- Where in your life can you leverage the money you are making?

- What opportunities can you think of to earn more?

- What investments have you thought of making?

- If you haven't invested, what's holding you back?

Make a plan to invest in a new area where you haven't before, or commit to a plan to invest for the first time. Give yourself a timeframe so you will really do it. Seek out a financial advisor if you need help. Simply investing $100 a month more in the same stocks that you already have and like could compound over time!

NETWORKING PREDICTS YOUR FUTURE

"In today's world, you have to interact.
You can't be some difficult, shy person
who is not able to look somebody in the face.
You have to present yourself.
You have to know how to talk about your vision,
your focus, and what you believe in."

—Anna Wintour

I had to join a mastermind group so I would have people to talk to.

When you start coming up and make a little bit of money, you stop getting invited to cookouts. You stop getting tagged on Facebook posts.

Your family starts in. "Man, you're moving too fast. You're greedy. Are you happy? Are your kids suffering?"

No, my kids aren't suffering. They're thriving in private school now because I bust my butt to give them the life that I didn't have.

I hired a coach because I wanted somebody to tell me when I was slacking and when I was coasting. I wanted someone to check me and ask if I slipped, "What's the matter with you?"

A coach holds you accountable. If you're finding it hard to work with a coach, that's all about you. You are making it difficult. Try to be coachable and drop your ego. Then see what happens.

Look at the five friends you hang around with the most. Are you friends with them because you want to be their friend, or are they in close proximity? Are you friends because you've simply known them your whole life?

It might be time to take stock of the people in your life if you are still hanging around that guy in high school who was your friend, but now you don't have much in common with him.

Part of the leveling-up process involves reassessing where you are spending your energy and time—or, more accurately, who is taking your energy and time from you.

COMMONALITIES MATTER

My hobbies have always been a conduit for networking. I know if I connect immediately with someone at a car meet that we have something in common, and I have networked and built businesses based on those car-club connections.

When I got into fitness, it made sense to align myself with others who were there and working on their fitness, too, because they were proving they were successful inside and outside of the gym. Our common ground would pay huge dividends for me down the road.

[
I joined a mastermind group so I could be with people who were successful in their businesses. Sure, I was eager to share what I had learned, but I was even more eager to soak up their knowledge.
]

I joined a mastermind group so I could be with people who were successful in their businesses. Sure, I was eager to share what I had learned, but I was even more eager to soak up their knowledge.

REACHING UP

I am always reaching up!

I refuse to be the big fish in a little pond.

I want to be pushed in all areas of my life, so reaching up to learn what I don't know and applying it to my life to improve it always made sense to me. Why would we not emulate what the big achievers in our world are doing?

When I needed to reinvent my networking circle, I simply moved to a different city and state. I'll say it again: "Your network is your net worth." I know this to be true.

A couple of years ago, I joined the Chamber of Commerce in the area where I live in Texas. I also joined the local Young Professionals' Group, which put on mixers and different community service projects.

Being in these circles took me out of my comfort zone, but it also forced my hand because I had to actively go out and seek and make new connections. Doing that opened up my sphere of influence to folks in my industry. These were people that I really wanted to get to know in North Texas.

When you're working with other power players, you can navigate those relationships and utilize the tools you learn about. It opens up new levels of networking. Some of those people became friends.

I'm not one who partakes in an abundance of social events, but I did see the advantages to spending my time at select events pretty quickly because, all of a sudden, I was dealing with the movers and shakers in my new area. I was dealing with people who were serious about being successful in their lives and in conducting their business, and when we decided to work together, we got right down to it.

TWO BIRDS, ONE STONE

Networking has allowed me to accomplish two aims at once. Sure, you will hang out with people in your industry, and you will have the chance to whip up mutually beneficial deals. But it also allows you to be around people who you aspire to be like.

My hobbies remove me from the company of people who are rude, lazy, dramatic, and toxic. I guess you could call that a cool side effect.

Hell, I just hired a new employee last year simply because I was wearing a Nike hat at the gym with our company logo on it. He saw that I was successful, and he wanted to be around the same types of people. He was reaching up, and that impressed me! Now, he has a job. Another benefit is that he already has the qualities I am looking for, so all I have to do is foster those God-given talents of his and get the hell out of his way.

I lost a lot of friends when I was going through my divorce because everyone always feels like they have to pick sides. I tried not to let myself get down about it, but it did sting. I also let it teach me something.

I chose to see the situation as a chance to reinvent myself, and, in my eyes, to part ways with people who weren't good for me. I didn't really like where I was at, anyway. I felt distant from my family, and, of course, that hurt, but doing that was ultimately what I needed to do to prepare for a brand-new life that has given me everything I ever wanted. Now, I am close to only 3-4 people who I talk to regularly. Sure, I have Facebook friends and other friends on varying social media platforms, but I don't mistake them for real connections.

MASTERMIND, ALREADY

I've joined Ryan Stewman's Break Free Academy and other mastermind groups.

Joining a mastermind group allows you to be around people who are positive and forward-thinking. It affects your life on every level and enlarges your circle with extremely influential people—who want to see you win! And guess what? You want the same for them. This mutually beneficial relationship might just be enough to shove you past your obstacles.

In the past, I have been haphazard about making friends. The friends I did have, didn't align with my business or leisure activities. I had to put thought into who I wanted in my circle and not just pick any random person. That said, please feel free to reach out to me and invite me into your circle. I would love to support you!

SOCIAL MEDIA FRIENDS ARE A MUST

When it comes to social media, you should consider joining Facebook groups. Geographically speaking, you can do more business with people and enlarge your circle of friends. I do prize in-person human connections over long-distance connections, but there is value in talking to people in any capacity and in all corners of the world.

The biggest thing we seem to be missing now is human interaction. The COVID-19 virus definitely shined a spotlight on how important it is to be in the company of the people you care about.

There are some definite drawbacks to a long-distance connection, however. When you send an email or message people, you lose some control over your tone of voice. I'm sure you've experienced this before. Intentions can be muted via online interactions versus the actual nuances of being in a face-to-face setting. So do both! In this day and age, connecting to people over multiple media is necessary to run a healthy and sustainable business. Consider it checking the box on a marketing must-do.

> *When you network in any capacity, you also repeatedly beat back the fear of speaking to other people.*

When you network in any capacity, you also repeatedly beat back the fear of speaking to other people.

You teach and re-teach yourself that reaching out to people doesn't kill you. Feeling awkward is not fatal. That's a fact. So, push yourself to do it, even block time on your calendar to hold yourself to it.

If you don't make a habit of putting yourself out there and doing what you are afraid of or simply dreading, you will become more and more anxious about taking those all-important leaps.

I used to be super uncomfortable speaking in front of large groups. But getting out of my comfort zone helped ease my social anxiety. The result was that my fear miraculously shrank. Now, I know I might have a few uncomfortable moments, but they are minimal when compared to the rewards that I reap from sharing my experiences in an effort to help people.

IT'S TIME TO CUT

Before you start cutting down your friends list, do something else first.

Address all the emotions that are going to bubble up around what you intend to do. Prior to cutting the cord, you are going to feel apprehensive. You are going to feel terrified. You are going to be insecure. Go ahead and feel all the feelings because it's vital to your mental health that you deal with those emotions. Don't bottle them up. Don't brush them to the side. *Deal* with them as they come.

If you're thinking, I*'m scared, Burton. I don't know if I can do this,* I want you to remember that scared equals "You are not going to do shit." This is why we have to work on beating back those fears, or at least reducing them to a state where you can face them and follow through.

If I'm scared, I know it's time to make the plan to finish what I started. I have to put my fear on the backburner and carry on no matter if I feel frozen or sick.

I recently finished a book called *Influence* by Robert Cialdini. Cialdini talks about how, when you're with people who you may have known for a long time, they will use that relationship against you. They know who you are, and they will have a hell of a time believing that you can change.

[
They're not weaponizing what you're doing. No, they'll come across as if they're trying to help you on your new journey.
]

They're not weaponizing what you're doing. No, they'll come across as if they're trying to help you on your new journey.

To make matters worse, you might not even realize that you are being manipulated because you've subconsciously programmed yourself to fall into the relationship dynamic that you are familiar with.

Let's say you've been a screw-up, and you suddenly decide you're going to get your shit straight. Maybe you're going to attend classes, do masterminds, or network. You feel really good about your decision. You feel empowered about it, but then someone else who has known you for a while does what they always do—try to break your spirit.

This is the relationship they know how to have with you. It's hard for people to raise their expectations to meet the new you. If things start to falter a little, and it seems that you are going off course, they might say, "Oh, well, when that doesn't work out, they have a job opening over here at my stepdad's place." When pressed, they would say they were helping you, but their response to you has to do with them. They aren't comfortable with you trying to scrabble your way out of the pot of crabs that are pulling you back in. In case you don't know what I am talking about, there is a phenomenon surrounding crabs. They really are crabby—and selfish. If one crab tries to crawl out of the pot to get away from being dinner, the others won't let it go. They stretch up and pull that escapee right back down into the pot with the rest of them. So, don't be a crab—and don't let a crab stop you!

That crab dynamic is really hard to get out of. It might even be rooted in codependence. There's a jostling for position when you make these monumental changes. What you are doing hits too close to home for some people.

[
How much time are you going to waste with people who don't want to help you?
]

How much time are you going to waste with people who don't want to help you?

If you don't think that's time mismanagement, I completely disagree with you.

When you get on a more successful road, stop for a minute and take a good look at your surroundings. If you expect to keep going and fulfill your goals, you will need people in your life who are going to support you. You will need people who will cheer you on instead of dragging you down. This is an area where you can't compromise because if you do, it is the same as shooting yourself in the foot. You won't be able to walk very far.

When you start taking risks, people might seem as if they want to protect you, but at the base of their intentions may be the fact that you are making them uncomfortable. When people get uncomfortable with your success, they want you to be like them, so you don't lose what you have in common. They might be afraid of losing you, too. It's not a good idea to hang out with people who want you to stay small to make themselves feel better and justify their excuses for not trying to do something with their life.

Is someone else's discomfort a reason for you to give up on your dreams? Of course not. In fact, their discomfort has nothing to do with you at all. It shouldn't be a message for you to do anything differently. No one gets permission to limit you. Even if you are uncomfortable with forging ahead with what you want to do, keep going! Growth is never going to be comfortable. As a leader, you are going to have to toughen up to make sure your boundaries stay intact, so you can continue to progress. You will need to have an intolerance for drama, too! Start practicing reinforcing your boundaries right now.

Will you be lonely, getting so specific as to who you allow in your life? Maybe. But being lonely is also better than being among people who would hurt you.

I'm not kidding. People who hold you back can affect your trajectory, your income, where you live, how motivated you are, etc. These are real impacts on your everyday life. That is what you are giving people who want to reign you in. You and I both know that is too high of a price to pay.

You might have to be super resilient for a minute, too, just until people get the message that you are serious about seeing yourself succeed and breaking personal records of achievement, even if it means distancing yourself from people or cutting them out of your life entirely.

Above all else, choose decisions that improve your life. And don't worry if other people think you opted for money over having a friendship with them. We both know you didn't.

[
Please let this sink in—there is nothing wrong withwanting an easier existence through having more money.
]

Please let this sink in—there is nothing wrong with wanting an easier existence through having more money.

Any 'friend' who claims you are choosing money over them doesn't want you to have it. Why would that be? What *real* friend wouldn't want you to have everything in your life that would make you happy? Being a good friend means hoping and wishing your friends will be happy, then doing everything in your power to make it happen—and vice-versa.

In addition to walking away from "friends," consider walking away from vices. I've found that when you're truly happy, you don't need vices.

The day I turned my back on drinking was the day my trainer said, "One alcoholic drink slows down your metabolism for 72 hours."

I looked him in the face, my jaw hanging, my eyebrows raised, then said, "Okay! That's not for me. No drinks for me!" He smiled as I said, "Let's get to work!"

The people around you who slug you on the shoulder and want to tip a beer or two are the people to beware of. I am not judging folks for wanting to enjoy alcohol responsibly. I am referring to people who have to drink every night because they are running from something. Their indulgences are a way of life. In fact, they get them through life, as sad as that is. When they stop drinking, they are forced to examine what they are doing and where they are going. Expect pushback from these people when you attempt to break away from the drinking culture, too. Know where their motivation is coming from. Even if you are emotionally mature enough to recognize this, and even if they are not a bad person, there is still no reason to keep them in your circle.

Before I extricate myself from any relationship, I always ask myself this telling question: *What values are they bringing to my life?*

You can also try: *Are they helping me get ahead?*

STDs are not what you think they are; at least, they aren't in *my* world. STD, to me, means Socially Transmitted Diseases, and it alludes to herd mentality.

In other words, people do what they allow others to persuade them to do. They jump on bandwagons, and the resultant toxicity spreads like a disease. You see it in people milking the system and making excuses for bad habits and addictions; you see it in money and relationship mismanagement; you see it in communities and neighborhoods where kids are forgotten, and crime is high. This toxicity becomes viral and extremely hard to cure when grown adults perpetuate it.

I want you to choose better.

If reading these words has been painful, maybe you can answer this question: *Why do you not want more for yourself?*

Why not experience the people who truly love you, celebrating the long miles you have gone to improve yourself and your life?

If you don't think it's possible to be among such friends, I can assure you, it is. At any one time, I can call the people who I have chosen to navigate life with and get nothing but support. I get nothing but honesty and encouragement. Having lived both sides of this coin, I will always choose my current network in lieu of the people who have betrayed me in the past.

I am here to share my pain with you so that yours might be lessened. I am here to lead you into finding the greatest version of yourself. I want that for you. Now, believe in yourself and reach out to the people who you believe will bless your life, as you will bless theirs.

While you're at it, make a list of the people who, right off the top of your head, you know are a drain on your life. Can you live without them? Should you live without them? If you are not ready for that step, can you create a little distance in the relationship, maybe interact with them on more of a surface level? You might not need to cut people out, but you very well could have to adapt the relationship to protect yourself and your dreams.

Next, I am going to share with you some of the deepest pain I have ever endured. As you read, please think about the painful times in your life and how you can use what you have been through as fuel to get ahead. This is why we experience pain: to let it teach and improve us.

I don't know about you, but when I think of pain in this way, it actually hurts less. Try it.

SECTION 2:
FINDING YOURSELF IN ALIGNMENT

CHAPTER: 8

I AM NOT WHO I WAS

"Dreams are the seedlings of reality."
—Napoleon Hill, Think and Grow Rich

When I decided to write this book, I realized that my childhood happened for a purpose. It is to show you that it doesn't matter where you start in life. And I know there are people who have had worse experiences. We are united through our pain and pleasure. We relate to each other through it. I am sharing my past with you so you can understand how I arrived in the place I am now.
Dreaming saved my life.

I should be a statistic.

It's a miracle I'm not homeless, an addict, or dead.

So many people I knew and am related to wound up that way.

Why not me?

I woke up. Thank God.

And I won't go back.

I fought for the life I have today, but I don't apologize for who I was, either. The joy of my life now is not an eraser of my past. I don't want to forget, and in many ways, I think I need to remember where I came from.

I came from the other side of the tracks, and I've never had anything handed to me on a silver platter (or any platter for that matter). I won't pave my road with bullshit and platitudes to get sympathy. I will only seek to gain a better understanding of who I am, where I came from, and what I have accomplished.

My mom and dad divorced when I was an infant, and being raised by a single mom was extremely difficult due to where we lived, how we lived, and life's circumstances. As a kid, everything was out of my control.

My parents divorced before I turned one year old. My mom moved us to Grove City, a suburb of Columbus, Ohio. She did the best she could, but a lot of bad decisions landed us in that location. I knew at a young age that there was something more to life than making money at a job that you don't like, just to get by. I wanted so much more than all the struggle that surrounded us.

In the middle of our tough life, my older brother John and I dreamed about the 1989 25th Anniversary Lamborghini Countach. He even had an iconic poster of it on the wall, and we would just stare at it. You know the one—the original supercar, white in color with the crazy body lines that screamed excessiveness and impracticality—I loved it! That V12 Italian bull literally moved my spirit, and now it literally moves my body when I drive my very own version of it.

John and I made a pact that someday, we would both own one.

Talking about that ride is burned into my memory. At the time, I think those cars cost about $100,000. Now, they're about $300,000.

One day when I was a little kid, I had a bright idea. I needed to make money. So I sat down and took some of my motocross magazines and cut out the pictures. I taped all the pictures into place on construction paper. I was simply making a collage, as little kids often do.

[
I didn't know it at the time, but I had created my very first product, and I was going to bring it to the marketplace!
]

I didn't know it at the time, but I had created my very first product, and I was going to bring it to the marketplace!

With my collage products in hand, I set out into the neighborhood, going door-to-door to sell my product for whatever I could get —a nickel or a quarter. I was about five or six years old and never even thought twice about what I was doing. I just knew I wanted to earn some money. Even though I didn't sell any of my collage products, I still managed to make a few bucks. I think my neighbors were impressed with my young entrepreneurial spirit and wanted to help me out.

But as I got older, no one wanted to encourage me to dream big—not when there were so many obstacles standing between me and my goals. Heck, I wasn't starting on an even keel. I came from the bottom and had a hell of a climb ahead of me, but, fortunately, I was blissfully unaware of my current environment, and it would be many years before I would come to the realization of how bad life could actually suck.

I didn't know living in a trailer park wasn't normal. I wasn't aware that it wasn't cool or that people made fun of them. I thought I was just like everyone else, part of a family trying to get by.

After the trailer park, my mom moved us to the city of Columbus and into a 1,200 square foot single-story, three-bedroom, one-bath home. It was the summer before fourth grade. She worked several jobs to make ends meet. My brother John was about seven years older than me and was living his own life. Our age differences kept us from having too much in common.

This new place was on the west side of Columbus, in the hood. Guns, drugs, and crime were all over the place, and shady people always hung around. People up to no good used their time for bad things that young boys shouldn't know about, let alone witness.

When I think of my childhood and compare it to my girls' lives, I'm floored. There wasn't much supervision. There weren't any parents scheduling in time to spend with me, other than my father, who would take me to football practice every night and who I spent every other weekend with, based on court orders. When I went out and roamed the streets, nobody knew what I was doing. I could have run into all kinds of trouble, and no one would have been the wiser.

Due to life circumstances, I grew up a lot faster than I should have. That was both a blessing and a curse. When I got older, I grew to appreciate life's challenges that had nearly killed me and others. An upbringing full of hardships will shape you into who you become. There is no way I could write this book without that mix of perspectives.

I remember once when Mom was pregnant with my sister. I was seven, and we were still living in the trailer park in Darby Dale, Ohio, just outside Grove City. My mom's husband at the time was a taxi driver named Kenny. He frequently came home drunk and would make a fuss around the house.

I can see this moment as clear as day. Mom had come in to read my evening prayers. I was in bed, tucked in for the night, trying to sleep after she had softly shut the door behind her.

The next thing I knew, I was jolted out of sleep by the loudest slap I had ever heard, and a crashing sound. I would later learn Kenny had smacked a plate and a cup of coffee out of my mother's hands, shattering it and staining the ceiling. The sound of a hand making contact with such brutal force that you can hear it in another room is something I'd rather forget, but never will.

When the yelling and fighting escalated, I sprang into action and leaped out of bed. As I raced out the door, I grabbed the metal Tonka toy truck that was on my bedroom floor. I ran out into the living room, and while Kenny's back was turned to me, I jumped up and cracked him in the back of the head so hard that he stumbled. Once he regained his composure, he started after me. I knew I'd hurt him, but with Kenny being so drunk, Mom shielded me from his advances and de-escalated the situation.

As for my real father, he was a good man trying his best to earn a living, I suppose. He is a Vietnam veteran, and to this day, he manages his demons mixed in with what I suspect is an undiagnosed bipolar disorder. I am the youngest of his three sons.

My father had a quick temper and ruled with a heavy hand.

Although he was firm, he was also fair, much like my grandfather, who'd passed on shortly before I was born.

My dad was a disciplinarian. He conditioned my mind to question which version of him was going to come through the door or pick me up for his allotted visitation time. I learned at a young age how to read people and became hyper-perceptive about how they carry themselves and their expressions, all thanks to my father. I had to stay ahead of him. I had to know where he was in his head and learn how to gauge how he was feeling, so I knew what to expect and what to avoid. My senses were quite fine-tuned at a very tender age. It was survival.

It's amazing that an instinct developed so young has become a vital asset today in my various businesses. I think my experiences with my father, which caused my hyper-perception, have improved my sales. I know they have helped me build relationships. I am attuned to people's non-verbal cues and can quickly size up a customer's or stranger's motives through a simple interaction with them.

If my dad was furious and intent on taking his bad day out on the rest of us, I knew I needed to get lost. If his expression was open, and he seemed friendlier and less prone to exploding, then a wave of relief would roll over me despite the continued need to walk on eggshells. I still don't know if some days he was all twisted up because he'd had a bad day at a job he hated, or what else could have caused his shift in moods. All I can say is that when he was in a good mood, my father, Jan, could be the most amazing, loveable, and kind human being. Maybe I am not meant to ever know why my father's moods shifted so often or so quickly.

As for my mother, I'm sure she detested her various jobs. She worked three of them when we moved to the city, including bartending at night, which kept her out until 3:00 AM some nights. I was lucky to see her three to four times a week, since she worked back-to-back-to-back hours.

Once she was at work, John, who was still in high school, sold cocaine and other drugs out of our home. People came and went at all times of the afternoon and night, when my mom wasn't around.

[
I thought to myself, Wow, he sure is popular! But it didn't take me long to figure out what was going on.
]

I thought to myself, Wow, he sure is popular! But it didn't take me long to figure out what was going on.

John was involved in other shady activities that caused people to come after him. So our house was a target. One of those times, my mom had been lying on the couch in between her work shifts when there was a drive-by shooting. The bullets came raining through the door, six to be exact. Two bullets ricocheted off the brass kickboard of the door, and one bullet flew into the sofa, missing my mother's head by mere inches. That bullet-wounded sofa still sits in the front window of my mom's house, to this day.

That's a moment I will never forget, and when it happened, I thought, *This is the life I don't want.* I can remember thinking those exact thoughts only a few times in my life, but that day is certainly branded in my mind as one of those few. Shortly after this incident, that little voice inside my head spoke again. I knew I wanted a different life, and that inner voice reassured me that there was hope, that my life was going to get better.

Looking back, I chose to hold onto the possibility that things would improve.

I didn't fully understand why the shooting had happened, nor did I know everything John had been up to, but he definitely had enemies—after all, it was the only reason our mom had almost died.

It took me until last year to tell my father about that drive-by shooting incident and explain to him a situation that had occurred later that same week. Both of those events had left me with a hurt so deep that I never told a soul about it—until one day when I finally broke down and confided in my wife what I had been harboring all those years.

When I was in fifth grade, I didn't have a lot of help with my schoolwork. No one was there to help, simple as that. Long division gave me worlds of trouble. I got a little behind in school and was stressing out because teachers were not aware of what was really going on. I was lost; I needed help, and I didn't have any. Truthfully, I didn't even know I needed a tutor (or that it was a viable option), and it obviously never registered with my parents, either. There were a lot of other things going on at home to deal with, so I guess I can see how my struggle in understanding dividends wasn't their first priority.

I had a big math test on Friday, the day after the drive-by shooting occurred. Suffice to say, less than 24 hours after watching that nightmare unfold— witnessing my mother jump from our couch while bullets tore through our home—I was unbelievably stressed out. And that's an understatement.

That Friday, I got the idea to cut school, which meant I would avoid the humiliation of failing that dreaded math test. Well, the school called my mom, so she knew I'd skipped, and that meant that my dad knew it, too. It was his weekend to have me, and it wasn't long after we pulled out of the driveway that he exploded with, "Why did you skip school?" As soon as the words were out, he close-fist backhanded me twice in the face.

I couldn't believe what had happened. He had turned on me so fast that all I could do was eat his fist—twice. "You don't ever skip school! That's not how we do things!" he yelled. All it took was two punches for me to hate my father.

I never objected or argued with my father, and I never tried to explain what had happened. I couldn't say a word with the taste of blood in my mouth while trying to choke back the tears rolling down my face. The *real* reason I had chosen to stay home was that I was officially living in the house of a drug dealer, and Mom had almost gotten shot to death while resting on the couch. I legitimately thought that if I spoke up, Mom and John would get into trouble.

I made the conscious decision to keep silent because the alternative to living with my mother was having to live with my father, and, in my mind, that wasn't ever going to happen again. It's odd to think back on this particular moment in my life when I chose to stay silent and live in a dangerous environment instead of living with my father.

Around that time, I ended up with stomach ulcers from worrying, while struggling to believe everything would be okay. I could feel it was, but at the moment when the pain hit me, it was hell on earth. I started throwing up blood.

No one believed me. My father thought I was a hypochondriac and wouldn't take me to the doctor because he assumed I just wanted attention.

This past year at Thanksgiving, I told my dad about why I'd skipped that day of school over 25 years ago. He still didn't get it. He got in my face and had the audacity to say, "You know you are to blame, too!" In my mind, I screamed back: I was 12!

That time in my life is surreal. I almost can't believe it was me living in that reality. What kind of life was that, anyway?

Life got even more surreal and tragic when John was murdered in his apartment in what I believe was a drug deal gone wrong, even though the police ruled it a suicide. "Street-justice," they called it. We buried John three days later, one day after what would have been his 19th birthday.

> ***His death stole the air from my lungs (it still does). I saw what his life had become and knew my odds of survival were slim.***

His death stole the air from my lungs (it still does). I saw what his life had become and knew my odds of survival were slim.

I had idolized John. He had single-handedly raised my younger sister, Rebekah, and me for those few crazy years when our mother worked all those hours. I wanted to be just like him—at least, in terms of the money I saw him bring home. If I was going to survive, I knew I had to claw and scratch my way out of that place even harder than before. After John died, I understood the gravity of living life the way he had, and that I needed a different direction.

Statistically, I should be in jail. I should be in that trailer park or back in West Columbus. I should be strung out on drugs, or dealing them. I should be in damaging, gut-wrenching relationships and have toxic people all around me.

I got out, and in addition to holding onto hope so tight to leave that life behind, I refused to believe that what happens to us defines us. I know the opposite is true: What we want, we get; we are who we tell ourselves we are. Our past and our treatment from other people have nothing to do with who we turn out to be. The external circumstances of our lives do not dictate our future. What does is our mindset—and that controls our actions, which, as we know, move us forward.

A lot of people cop out and use what happens to them and how they grew up as an excuse. That's *why* they do drugs. It's *why* they go to jail *and* end up in abusive relationships or perpetrate abuse on others. It's *why* they can't get ahead. Their car constantly breaks down, they're cheated on or lied to, and so on. These excuses prevent their forward motion.

What I want has everything to do with my inner drive.

I will literally kill myself working too hard.

That's why I had to institute rules to reign in my fire.

Without them, I will get up earlier, stay up later, work harder and do whatever it takes until I am dead in the ground.

Since I wasn't ready for an early grave, I decided to follow a   specific set of rules that you are reading about in this book.

Anytime I have ever gone after anything significant for myself, the drive to succeed had to come from within me. I didn't have a lot of external pressure. No one expected anything from me, and I didn't have a lot of support.

Every goal I chased was intrinsic and internal. When I got a little bit older and matured, the face I saw staring back at me made me feel like a winner.

One day, with my face reflected in the mirror, I resolved that I would only be a high achiever and never a mediocre striver, no matter if I was talking about my career or being a father.

It helps that I have always wanted to win, that winning is important. But again, this kind of drive and mentality is a definite double-edged sword. My insane drive is present and nagging all the time. It scolds me when I feel I am slacking, and, as you can imagine, I am very hard on myself. The idea of failing and landing myself back in that trailer park isn't an option. So I have to be super strict with myself!

When I was a kid, my mom had a framed painting depicting an old brick Victorian mansion with a Rolls-Royce parked out front. At the bottom, in bold print, it read, "My tastes are simple. I like to have the best." That was and is the mindset and life I want. I started young. My mother is a dreamer, too; she just never realized how much was in her own control.

While you may not have an intrinsic drive, you do have the ability to make up your mind. You do have the ability to make choices, and in the end, that is all you need to have if you want it all.

You can decide how you perceive every event in your life, even the ones that take you to your knees. You can choose to see disappointment as the sign to find new solutions.

So many people don't understand that they are the ones standing in their own way, and I don't say this with judgment. I say this to let you know that I did it; and that the only way out—to achieve liberation and happiness—is to find that silver lining no matter how dark the clouds surrounding it may appear.

Once I discovered this, my life, habits, and trajectory all changed for the better.

I hope you use what I learned to make your life what you want it to be and change it for the better. That's one of the reasons I wrote this book, after all.

PREPARE FOR ALIGNMENT

**"The person who said,
'Winning, isn't everything,' never won anything."
—Unknown**

The rest of this book covers the epiphanies that have struck me in applying the Six Assets of Alignment in my life. It's not enough to share the tactics that work for me to keep everything rolling in the same direction. You need to be prepared to succeed—and for your car to hit the occasional pothole.

You will want to address these considerations on your journey to Alignment:

- The Demons Want to Take It All – Finally and permanently, beat back your demons, which are your negative thoughts.

- Rejecting Outside Validation – You need only look inside yourself to find everything you need to succeed.

- You Don't Have to Hate Work – It's true! There are people alive and well who love what they are doing.

- Knowing Yourself – It's time to be truthful about who you are and what you need.

- You Are as Good as Your Support Team – We all need cheerleaders and people we can count on in our lives.

- Called for More – What are you truly called for, and why are you here? Figure that out and honor it, and your life is set!

- Relentless, Not Ruthless – It is not talent or innovation that will win. It is a never-say-die attitude that will outwork anyone else.

- Too Many Gifts – Don't shy away from your talents. You were given them for a reason—to put them to use.

- Be the Best No Matter What – Nothing feels better than having no regrets about how you execute your tasks!

- Following Your Plan – You need to know where you're going, or you could end up anywhere—or nowhere.

- Pivoting – Learn how to react when you must make a decision. Life will always be full of surprises, good and bad.

- Achieving in Hardship – It's not what you think—hardship doesn't have to end you. You can still thrive in the most grueling of times.

- Appreciation and Alignment in Your Life – Gratitude directly feeds into the quality of our lives and the opportunities that complement our alignment.

- Defining Your 'Why' – This will help you in your moments of fear and will eliminate the doubt in your decisions!

- How the Six Assets of Alignment Connects to Your 'Why' – Everything is tied together. Your actions in integrity in the six key Assets stem from the reason you do what you do, your 'why.'

- You Deserve It All – It's easy to read, hard to accept.

- Self-Improvement – We always need to push ourselves for more. Besides, it's fun learning what we can accomplish, as well as it ties into hitting our larger goals.

- Reassess Periodically – Plans get stagnant, too, as do goals. When energy and enthusiasm are lost, promises and dreams go by the wayside.

- Time, Out of Thin Air – Let me teach you a trick about living two days in one.

- Excellence Everywhere – How you take the high road in one asset is how you should apply that to the other assets

- Making Money – Naturally, we need to talk about it, but most people think of 'money' as a dirty word. Let's focus on earning it, making plans to maximize our profits, and putting our money to work—to make more!

Of course, you can hop around from subject to subject in whatever order you want so you get the most out of this book. That's the goal. Take some time and think about what these considerations mean to your life.

HOW DO YOU WANT YOUR LIFE TO BE?

In the Introduction, I asked you about the three things in your life that you wanted to change. Now, I want to know (and you need to answer honestly, even if it requires a lot of work)—*How Do You Want Your Life to Be?*

This is an important question, and it rests on the intention that you are charged with creating.

It is easy to read this book without absorbing the words. I want you to understand the content and then take action. Answer the questions that need your clarity. You must know before figuring out *how* you want your life to be why you want it that way.

Then you need to know who you are living your life for.

Has it occurred to you that you might not necessarily be living for yourself?

If you have a family, you know where I'm coming from. There are little people and, potentially, a partner to take care of and contribute to. But did you forget to make plans to take care of yourself?

If you're like most people striving for more, the answer is probably, yes.

Yet, if you're not happy with yourself and where you're at, how can you begin to love and take care of the most important people in your life?

You can't.

Or maybe you are taking care of your family, but you don't love it. Are you feeling "burned out," as if you're working too many hours?

[***Do you sense resentment simmering around the edges of your life because you are being pulled in too many directions?***]

Do you sense resentment simmering around the edges of your life because you are being pulled in too many directions?

There's a difference between just 'going through the motions' and doing your part while taking care of your priorities.

You know that the people closest to you deserve your best.

This is why we have to take care of ourselves. If we don't, we won't be able to serve from a place of gratitude.

Without gratitude, life is dry and boiled down to what we *have* to do and not *what* we want to do.

Do you see the difference?

In case you're wondering if there are any connections between what we do and the joy we feel in our relationships—there are!

Your mind might already be spinning, and if it is, I urge you to spend some more time in this section to answer the questions here.

You are going to get to know yourself quite well as you read this book because it's *necessary* to make the lifestyle changes centered in the Six Assets of Alignment.

And it is even more necessary to hold firm when there are forces outside your control ready to sabotage your progress.

THE DEMONS WANT TO TAKE IT ALL

'Demons' are our destructive thoughts.

They lurk in each of the six Assets our lives revolve around—ready to confuse us and take our essence away in Mindset, Faith, Family, Fitness, Finances, and Network.

[*Demons are our destructive thoughts.*]

Sometimes demons look like self-sabotage or doubts. They might even be disguised as laziness or fear. One fact is certain: If you don't learn how to tame them, they will take huge chunks of your life away from you and leave you lonely, broke, frustrated, disappointed, and heartbroken over every loss.

Don't fret. When we are done here, the demons won't stand a chance against you.

Here's an example of how a demon might show up in your relationships: Think back to when you first got together with your spouse or partner. Now ask yourself (and answer honestly, even if it scares you): Did you get into your current relationship to help your significant other or yourself? Even if you love the person, did the thought cross your mind that they could help you somehow? Did you stumble across the idea that you could help them and that it would make you feel good about yourself? Did you choose them so you wouldn't be alone? When people talk about taking on a person as a project, this is what they mean. Do you see yourself here?

Getting to the bottom of these questions doesn't mean your marriage or relationship is over. It doesn't mean if it's in trouble, it can't be salvaged. You need to know the truth, so you have the knowledge to solve effectively whatever's wrong.

I think you can agree with me that reading that paragraph may have stirred some internal analysis that didn't feel so good—keep in mind that not all self-reflection will do that. We don't want to consider that we might have married or connected with people for the wrong reasons.

If you identified with that paragraph, though, I don't want you to worry. And when I speak of relationships, I want to be clear. The people in your circle can change. We know this often happens. People come in and out of our lives. The goal isn't to try and achieve perfect relationships with other people. Yes, we should always be as kind and loving as possible. The goal is to have the best relationships with ourselves, so we can create a place of perfect acceptance for others. Even if the members of your circle rotate in and out, it doesn't mean you don't have a family. Keep telling yourself that there are plenty of people around you who love you. It's true.

As you strive for success, not everyone will be thrilled for you. Some might be threatened and use all kinds of reasons as a defense to criticize what you are doing in trying to improve yourself. They may also make up reasons to distance themselves from you. That's okay. It hurts, but it's okay. You can't prepare for how others will react to your success, even those closest to you. And how people respond to you might really surprise you. This is another demon you have to confront and stare down until it disappears.

When it comes to love, you might struggle for a few years or mates or dates until you get it right. Too many times, I've been the right guy for the gal, but she wasn't the right one for me. Again, that's okay. I'm happy I can see the truth and work toward making better decisions. That's the kind of person I am. I make my choices and sometimes even make mistakes in public, in front of everyone. I don't expect you to be perfect, and I don't expect me to be, either. I just want both of us to try as hard as we can.

Everyone has demons they are constantly working through, and I have learned that those pesky creatures lie waiting, dormant, until the time is "right" to turn us onto a destructive path. Whatever the reasoning behind these demons and no matter what they want, whether it is reassurance, freedom, validation, love, etc.— we feed *them*. It doesn't require a ton of thought to do so, either. Feeding them is usually instinctual and done with very little premeditation. All we know is that we want the destructive, self-loathing, and demeaning thoughts to 'get the hell out of Dodge.' These kinds of thoughts are the definition of self-persecution. But we will do anything to silence these demons, even make tons of bad decisions that will hurt both ourselves and the people we love.

Demons don't just occur in our relationships; they pop up everywhere in our lives.

I am prone to depression and self-deprecating thoughts. That's a demon of mine. I refuse to feed it and choose not to drink alcohol. I want and need absolute clarity and control of my mind. I still actively battle demons like these in my life on a daily basis. I share this with you in the hope that you, too, can be honest about the negative thoughts that you experience. That you can feel more comfortable and less freaked out about having demons and naming them.

When we give into these destructive thoughts and allow ourselves to develop negative personas, we literally go against God. As I look back on my life, and especially in writing this book, I can see that I easily turned my back on Him. For a long time in my life, I actually put the care and feeding of my demons ahead of showing God my love and devotion.

REJECTING OUTSIDE VALIDATION

Until I came to grips with what I was meant to do, I was caught in a vicious cycle of what I *should* do (according to the people around me) versus what I needed and wanted for my life. This ignited a massive inner battle and anxiety. How I handled that situation was all wrong for me.

I wasn't seeing myself. I was trying to be like everyone else because they told me that kids like me didn't go far or amount to much. I could practically hear their reasoning in my head: *Be like us, and we'll finally accept you.*

I'm not going to lie; thinking I could be accepted when I had felt like an alien all my life was tempting.

But living like this will kill you quicker than anything because **conforming is just another way to die**. Have you allowed yourself to settle into a job you hate or put yourself into a box that doesn't permit you to reach your full potential and/ or desires? Well, I did, and I paid the price heavily, but fortunately, I was able to save myself.

First, I had to reject the notion that I needed anyone else's validation.

YOU DON'T HAVE TO HATE WORK

The majority of Americans hate their jobs. This is one hell of a sad truth to me. If you feel this way, you might think, *What am I supposed to do?*

As young adults, we learned that we are supposed to earn a living by taking Column A (income) and subtracting from it Column B (expenses). What's left should equal a positive number. We set ourselves up to believe this is our best-case scenario—just getting by in a job we hate.

Here's another ridiculous truth: We think that staying in a job will be fine because the longer we work, the more we are supposed to make. But in truth, it won't matter how much money you make. When you hate working a clock, you feel discouraged and dead inside.

We also know living the majority of our lives doing what we hate leads to depression. Depression is a silent killer no one likes to talk about. So why do people stay? Are they caving into the need for security, thereby spawning situational depression, or are they aggravating clinical depression?

Consider this: What if your depression and anxiety could go away through a career change? Wouldn't that make it worth it to embark on your journey to major life changes?

I can sense the hesitation in you. These are big decisions to make. We all pause for a minute when we think about upending our lives, but what if our fear could go away, too? It might make you feel better to know that I have met many people who started off as anxious or depressed, who then learned how they were living didn't align with their goals and dreams, and when they made a change, their entire lives improved!

[*Did you know that being complacent is a form of negative thinking?*]

KNOWING YOURSELF

We have to dissect our lives and figure out the 'WHY' in our day-to-day actions while setting fear aside. The good news is that I can help you with that, too.

To get started, ask yourself the following, and be sure to answer honestly:

- *Why are you living this way?*

- *Why have you surrounded yourself with certain people?*

- *Why have you settled on your current job?*

- *Are you happy?*

- *What are your core values?*

If you're struggling to identify your core values, maybe you've never really pondered them. Perhaps you've inherited values from your parents/family/home life and are now fighting to define them as an adult.

It's never too late to reevaluate and make decisions for yourself. It's also never too late to evaluate the medication you are on for your depression or anxiety. I used to take medication, and now I don't. It nearly killed me. I won't touch it.

Please understand that when I talk to you about taking medication for depression and anxiety, I am not speaking about true clinical depression and anxiety. I am simply stating that oftentimes we find ourselves at the tail end of a series of oppressive choices—and we might not even realize what we are doing. We might just listen to our doctors without questioning them.

Regardless of whether we are medicating or not, we singlehandedly can place our lives in a rut that we will struggle to get out of. This is why it is vital to remember that things don't happen TO us—they happen *BECAUSE OF* us.

I shared my deepest, darkest moment to explain where I have been and to let you know I never want to go back there.

But running from my pain won't keep me safe. Knowing exactly where I went wrong on my path, will. I have to accept it, and I do. I encourage you to do the same with the hardest moments of your life.

In this book, I help you spend time on what to do versus what not to do, on how to build upon the good habits that you need to practice in your life to get to the point you want to get to.

The reason I share this all with you is that living my life by the Six Assets of Alignment has expanded my mind. It's like a gap opened up, and I can feel the light streaming in and enlightening me.

As it enlightens me, I know I am not alone, that none of us are ever meant to feel abandoned. We need people to fill many positions in our lives.

YOU ARE AS GOOD AS YOUR SUPPORT TEAM

Let's talk for a minute about the importance of having a support team behind you.

Your support team can be your family, but it certainly doesn't need to be. We don't all have close family members. Sometimes, fights or other events happen, and people grow apart. Your support team can be made up of friends, mentors, co-workers, and whoever wants to go to bat for you and help lift you up instead of tear you down.

Let me ask you:

- *Do you have a coach?*

- *Do you have someone you can confide in?*

- *Do you have someone who is excited to see you succeed?*

I don't often discuss my first marriage, as it ended in failure, but looking back, I can see that it wasn't the right fit. When things got tough, I was alone. Of course, I contributed to this. I was egotistical, and my head was filled with defensive thoughts. I felt rejected and hated any kind of perceived weakness on my part— which I now know can be plainly explained as vulnerability. That hatred of who I was and what I was feeling nearly led to my permanent destruction.

I relied upon the validation of other people—what I now know was co-dependency that came from much-repeated trauma, beginning in my childhood.

The second that someone doubted me, I came out emotionally swinging. I didn't have the deep core confidence needed to succeed, and I knew no matter what I went after, I would fail.

Right before I hit my blackest days, I was trying to accomplish a major goal because, if I hit it, it meant I had worth and that I could trust my instincts to direct my life. It meant I was tough and could hang in there. This is why I had to succeed despite everyone around me trying to put me in chains. It was why being in those chains was torture and ate away at my mind, why it contributed to the days when I fought for my next breath.

Can you imagine how much farther I would be in life if I'd had a support system under me much sooner? I wouldn't have been swallowed up by the shadow side of myself.

> *When I finally woke up enough to make changes, after feeling enough agony to last me a lifetime, I flipped my self-narrative.*

When I finally woke up enough to make changes, after feeling enough agony to last me a lifetime, I flipped my self-narrative.

Instead of raking myself over the coals and shredding my self-esteem, I shut all that out. I thought, instead: *What are my strengths? What can I really focus on?*

Then I was ready to move on.

Before you move on, keep getting to know yourself…

Ask yourself:

What do I want?

Go deep now: What do you envision your life to be? I don't mean blurting out a meaningless phrase like "I want to make a lot of money." That doesn't tell you anything.

You are a unique individual. What do you want to do differently? What is your highest and best use of your life? What actions do you need to take to support that?

Are you trying to do things your own way all the time? Are you open to the messages or signs that are showing you what you are capable of? The times when you nail that project, and it's easy? The people who come to you for help? Pay attention and open your eyes to see all your options.

Consider these questions and be honest about your actions:

- *Why am I taking these actions?*

- *Why am I in this career?*

- *Why am I in this relationship?*

- *What are my true goals?*

- *What are my core values?*

- *Do they align with my goals?*

- *Where do I want to change and why?*

- *When I think about being happy in Mindset, Faith, Family, Fitness, Finances, and the Network Assets of my life, where does my mind immediately go?*

When you give yourself clarity on those questions, you will be all set to learn about the secrets of alignment.

YOUR TRAJECTORY

"I keep wondering—how many people do you need to be before you can become yourself?"
—Unknown

CALLED FOR MORE

For whatever reason, I was always a dreamer. Even as a young boy, I knew there was something more for me. When everything was so bleak, and I was living amidst violence and poverty, I was still a very happy-go-lucky dreamer. That was God's gift to me: allowing me to always see something greater. When I look back, I recognize I was favored by Him. He let me know there was more for me.

I was even given a noble name that only reinforced that fact: Burton Prescott Hughes.

I know now that name wasn't an accident. People have made fun of my whole life because of it, and they made fun of me because I was different. When I was a kid, everyone was like, "You think you're sweet?" People judged me for what I couldn't control. It was weird. As a kid, I didn't have many tools to handle that type of bullying, so I let it eat at me.

Going around and living your life when you don't think you have much on the inside is pretty sad and depressing. People didn't see the real me. That's why I worked so hard to keep a smile on my face all the time. A simple smile can tell people a lot. I focused on putting that warmth out there, so people could see past the preconceived notions of my exterior.

I also have the ability to look into someone and see their heart and their feelings. If they're sad, I know. I'm very perceptive and excellent at reading people. So I focus my efforts on this, using it as a tool to help people as I am serving them in their work.

RELENTLESS, NOT RUTHLESS

Tim Grover, the author of the best-selling book, *Relentless*, said, "We're born relentless, taught to relent." That is true for those of us who are a different breed and refuse to settle. When I heard that, I was fixated on what it meant for me. I must have sat there for an hour struck by it because it's so true.

I remember trying to come out of my shell and my dad saying, "Sit down and shut up! Don't be seen." When you hear that often enough, you come to believe this is how your life is meant to be. That's what I meant when I said my dreamer mentality saved my life. I used it to escape hurtful words and survive, to create my own reality when the environment I lived in was stifling.

When you come from nothing, the survival tactic is to blend in. You don't want to stand out because when you do, people throw stones at you. It's easier for most people to fade into the woodwork. Standing out and winning puts pressure on you. Then you have to do it again. So most people will play small. If you play small, you live in the gray. You also won't know anyone on top. It's safe in the gray.

We've all heard the saying that, "You are who you hang out with." That's a paraphrase of the original, but you get the idea. And it's true: Hang out with people on the bottom, and I promise you will stay there.

> *If you want to resist the kind of life you don't want, you have to get uncomfortable being in places you're not used to.*

If you want to resist the kind of life you don't want, you have to get uncomfortable being in places you're not used to.

You have to be relentless in changing your environment. You have to be relentless in helping people to change their perception of you (once you have changed your perception of yourself, of course).

I always wanted to be the best and dress the best, so people would see me as more than a product of my circumstances.

In my child's mind, I thought, *If I look good, I feel good. If I look good, I will do a better job.*

I was only in third grade when I started thinking about my life like that. (The relentless gene starts working early, I guess.)

TOO MANY GIFTS

When I was young, I was told that I socialized too much, and, after a while, I got into trouble. I now know the trouble came from my gifts. I am energetic, outgoing, and I love to meet new people. Those were my gifts that were being squashed.

When I heard I was too talkative, I stopped talking. (My epiphanies about how I was actually gifted in talking would come later.) When I stopped talking, teachers and other adults told me I was depressed. Once they diagnosed me, then they challenged me: "Why don't you stand out? Why don't you try?"

After hearing that, I had no idea what to do because when I tried to be myself, I was labeled egotistical, an elitist—yes, even as a kid living in a trailer park! Grownups and kids gave me all these labels when I was just trying to get along. As a youngster, I was so confused. It was hurtful knowing that who I was, wasn't accepted. Of course, I shriveled up. Any kid would.

I couldn't win, either way. Damned if I did, and damned if I didn't. Where does a kid even go from there?

After a long time of being silent and making yourself small, so no one sees you, you start telling yourself: *This is it for me.* I stopped dreaming.

Maybe you have stopped dreaming, too? Maybe you have a similar story that you can't forget that causes you to play small. The good news is that you can see it. And you want to change. I know if you can see it, you can be it—because I was in your same shoes.

I also know if you keep going on that path and settling to make other people happy, then your whole life will be set up for failure. You will marry the wrong person, take the wrong job, file for bankruptcy, and fall on hard times. You will feed the chaos in your life as you do nothing about it.

I lost a decade because I tried to live small – all because I went against my God-given talents.

Settling is why women stay in relationships with violent men, just like my mom did. She was married 11 times, so there was always a mean, drunk, and abusive stepfather in my house. My mom was attracted to alcoholics like her dad. But I don't hold it against her. In retrospect, I can understand why she made these decisions. She honestly thought that was what she deserved.

My mom's dad was a drunk who died of cirrhosis of the liver. He was an asshole, sorry to say. I look back, and I know my mom could have changed if she'd wanted it badly enough, but she settled.

If you're stuck in a nine-to-five job that's not commission or incentive-based, you might think that's all you should have, too. We've all read the stories of people who have worked at a company for 30 years, who started at the same time with another guy and then, 30 years later, the one guy's the president of the company, but the other dude's middle management. That's because one person took the opportunity to excel. They decided that they deserved more.

Or maybe the other guy didn't know how to control their gifts, either?

Maybe they were also told to 'tone it down?'

BE THE BEST NO MATTER WHAT

I'll let you in on my trick that I've used to get recognized in the workplace and move up the professional ladder.

Whether I was out knocking on doors with our roofing company or cleaning as a janitor, I've always challenged myself. Now, these are considered to be some of the 'lowest level roles' in a company, but if you are doing them, do what I did. When I was the janitor, I told myself I was going to clean to the best of my ability because I was going to prove my worth—since you get paid what you're worth. And it works!

When you do your best, people take notice and decide you are ready for more.

Also, instead of pissing and moaning about your job, be grateful that you have one. But don't be grateful for the circumstance—that's the difference. You might have to play the role that you're in at this moment because that's your life right now (and that's okay, temporarily). But why not absolutely kill it in the position you're in so that other people will notice?

If you need to be to work at a certain time in the morning, show up a little earlier; get that competitive edge and sharpen it. Stay a little later and work harder. Approach your job like you're the CEO of your position. I don't have to tell you that this is all a mindset shift. Sure, you're doing a job you hate, but make it the best it possibly can be as you tell yourself, *I am not staying here.* People who master their jobs move up.

Do this, and turn on that new mindset. Before you know it, there will come a time when you won't even recognize yourself in the mirror. I didn't recognize myself.

In 2006, I looked myself in the mirror and asked: *What are you doing? Where are you right now?* As I looked back at my reflection, I knew I wasn't going to settle anymore. I wasn't going to listen to everyone else discouraging me. They didn't know me! I went back to my old dream, more determined than ever to get everything I wanted.

Even if you've been stuck for 15 years, what you've wanted is still there. You just need a kickstart to get going.

I had to take the deepest dive inside myself to get to where I am today. That meant holding myself accountable, so I could really see how I was showing up in all my relationships.

If you think I'm too money-focused, understand that money can't buy confidence. When I got on the road to getting myself back, I learned that quickly.

TRICK YOURSELF INTO SUCCESS

You can almost trick yourself into success by attacking other areas of your life. If you're in a relationship and it's leaving a lot to be desired, as long as you're safe (if you're not, get out right now), go back in time to when you were in love with each other. What was going on then? How were you giving your partner attention? What was it that you were originally drawn to? If you are not settling, you can rekindle what you had because it's actually still there, deep inside. Of course, sometimes you can't rekindle, and that's okay, too.

You might be thinking, *Burton, you don't understand—we have three kids, and my wife does this or that* thing. It's not about what your husband or wife is doing: How are you participating in the relationship? What are you doing now that you weren't doing before, and vice-versa?

When I was a trainer, I met a lady in a gym class who wanted to lose weight to be more sexually desirable to her husband. She took ownership of her situation and tried to correct it. She held herself accountable and did what she could to improve things. Simple as that.

The best way to make the improvements that you want in your life is to focus on yourself. It's okay to be self-centered as long as you don't get carried away. If you want to take good care of yourself, you need to be self-centered, or it's not going to work. Doing this allows you to grow.

That kind of growth has a positive snowball effect on every Asset. The happier you are, the more money you will make, the easier your life will be.

[
Above all, make sure you work on your mindset because a negative mindset can't reap a positive life.
]

Above all, make sure you work on your mindset because a negative mindset can't reap a positive life.

You are where you are in life because of the decisions you've made. There's a reason you're sitting in that cubicle. You gave up, or you settled, period. You need to accept it. Don't dwell on it, but do change it.

That's the one fact we all need to realize about our lives: They can change at any minute. You can demand something different. Commit to being either all out or all in.

When I was working for a building company and then got my real estate license, my co-workers at the real estate office kept their doors open to talk to each other. I saw this and thought, *Yeah, I'm not here to make friends. My door is going to stay shut. I gotta work.* I decided I would be friendly, but that I had enough friends. My path was not going to walk itself.

In that first month, I sold 12 houses. It fed my 'why' and my motivation and Aligned seamlessly with my six Assets.

I wasn't playing around anymore. I was paying attention. I wasn't going to be one of the people I saw winging it their entire lives.

On the subject of money and not being able to afford what you want, tell yourself the same thing Grant Cardon says: *"No, it's not that it's expensive. I just don't make enough money."* When you do this, you put the responsibility back on you, which also allows you to solve the problem. I still use this technique.

I no longer have a scarcity mindset. I always try to look for the best and give myself the best. I make what I want to happen because I know I have the power to do so.

My life is by design because I choose it to be.

[*My life is by design because I choose it to be.*]

FOLLOWING YOUR PLAN

If there's a pothole in your lane and you're heading toward it in your aligned car, it doesn't mean you can't avoid it. You can stay in your lane and dodge what comes at you. Don't be so structured that you can't pivot and make changes 'on the fly' for the better.

Definitely stay the course, but when you need to get out of the way—move!

Draw a line in the sand. Tell yourself that you will not look like you do anymore. You will not drink alcohol anymore. You will not give into anger anymore. Whatever your goals are, get serious and do not back down from them.

Focus on yourself first. That's mindset. In the section about the Six Assets of Alignment, I talk about that topic first. The simple truth is that you can't do anything else in your life if you haven't made up your mind to do it—and you can't even get that far if you haven't worked on your mindset consistently.

You have to change what you expect, to get what you truly want.

Are you going to put shitty, dirty gas in your car? No.

Are you going to keep a Rolls-Royce clean? Absolutely, you are. You have to maintain it. Picture someone driving down the road in a dirty Rolls. It doesn't make sense.

Why would you own a car like that if you aren't going to take care of it?

Your life and how you live are no different. We see people who are killing it in business, but they're drunks. We've read of massive moguls who cheat incessantly on their wives.

That's not okay for them, and it's not okay for you.

A grown man came up to me the other day after he had listened to my speech. He was crying and saying, "That really spoke to me. I cheated on my spouse." I looked at him for a brief moment and asked, "Do you feel bad about it?" That's when the excuses rolled out. "My wife, this and that—" I said, "It sounds like you don't feel bad about it. Is that because you're emotionally done?" He told me that he was cheating because his wife was on his back all the time. He was seeking something else. But before that conversation, he hadn't given much thought as to why he was doing what he was doing and how he was contributing to the chaos in his life.

Obviously, I don't condone cheating, but I can understand why people say they do. The disconnect is, if that's your life, then make sure that you take ownership of what you are doing and make the right decision to live in Alignment with what you want.

If you're settling and can't move forward, that's one thing, but if you're leaving because you don't want to do the work and it's easier for you, that's not okay. You also can't be in a relationship if you are the only one trying to heal your partnership. If you want different things in life, then maybe parting is best if that other person will drag you down. If you're an ocean liner and they're an anchor, it's going to be difficult and more than likely won't work out.

But, if you can, and the love is still there, save your relationship.

You don't want to simply go through life. "You want to grow through life," as Eric Butterworth said, so stop going through the motions.

It might be a little easier for me to regard life as so black and white because of my upbringing.

I know now that how I was raised was the wrong way. I would never raise my children like that!

After I grew up and went through the defining and painful times I did, I found my correct path and set everything right. I was then able to move forward to have my own family.

I don't judge myself for my past, either. I know, as a kid, the situation I was in was out of my hands.

Moving forward and parenting my beautiful daughters has been massively healing.

That's what life is about: making it better, healing. Do more for the people in your life and leave a legacy you can be proud of.

Start by going to BurtonHughesOfficial.com and downloading the Align Your Empire app today.

CHAPTER: 11

ASSETS CAN SAVE YOUR BUSINESS

"Hope smiles from the threshold of the years to come,
whispering it will be happier."
—Alfred Lord Tennyson

I made my business pandemic-proof before there was even a pandemic.

If you are a small business owner, this chapter is a must-read to nurture your innovation and persistence.

PIVOTING: 2020 WAS SUPPOSED TO BE THE YEAR OF PERFECT VISION

At the end of 2019, people were talking about how the flu season was going to be something else this year. They were really pushing that flu vaccine.

I'm not one to get caught up in the fervor. I acknowledge. I listen. I'm aware. But I am also a creature of habit and stick to my schedule.

So, when we first started hearing about COVID-19, and when Trump put a mandate on all incoming international travel, that's when everyone said, "Maybe there's something more going on?" There was a lot of uncertainty. The markets were getting crazy. Between the impeachment, the hype about the flu, and COVID-19, the groundwork was laid: Something big was looming.

As I said, I'm very structured. I find comfort in living by a schedule because it keeps me accountable. And I still make sure that every day I'm on offense. But during the COVID-19 pandemic, there was a lot of uncertainty.

I got a crash course in handling uncertainty on a smaller scale at the end of 2008/ early 2009 with the financial crisis. But we weren't fully locked down back then. As a realtor, I got to the point of waiting on a bunch of deals to close with the bank and then hearing, "Oh, sorry, we are no longer solvent. The bank that had your loan isn't available anymore." People who had literally sold their home on

Sunday and were supposed to close on their new house on Monday were out of luck. That's how fast it happened. They had sold their house and had their U-Haul packed up, but they had no new house and couldn't move into their old house because it had sold.

I was their realtor, and they asked me, rightfully so, "What do you mean, the loan program isn't available? What are you talking about? We were clear to close." I was very much in uncharted territory then. But I'm a great problem solver, so I never got too rattled.

Because of that time, I felt prepared to go through COVID-19, in a way—even though the circumstances were completely different.

Despite that, there are still a lot of similarities. In 2020, life felt out of our control. We know we all do better when we are in control. Like anyone else, I had to have normalcy, so I dug into my schedule hard to do what worked for me. As the US was shutting down and refusing to admit any people from out of the country, the mandates worsened to not allowing people to travel from state to state.

The next thing you know, you couldn't go to restaurants. You couldn't go to bars. Places were closing for two weeks at a time. We seemed to adapt. It was weird, but it was also only two weeks, and the barrel we were staring down wasn't that long.

Thankfully, I had stayed pretty busy throughout the year—and made sure I had planned for the future. (This is something you always need to do—so make sure you commit to it.) For me, it was business as usual because I had done the work the previous three months, and more work was coming in.

Two weeks turned into six weeks. At the beginning of April, we heard that government lockdowns were happening, and many people figured that would last another six weeks. We were now staring at eight weeks.

That's when the fear crept in. People got scared. Companies made massive slashes to their staff. On the second day of the two-week mandate, Grant Cardone put a 90-day freeze on all the dividend payments and real estate investments that were supposed to go to his employees. People who had invested their life savings or sold their homes were out of luck. If you had sunk $100k into the company and were expecting to get monthly income from it, that didn't happen. But he wasn't the only one pulling the rug out from under people. Job loss affected the entire country.

Mastermind groups were canceled. In my mastermind group, we no longer had meetings. We did virtual get-togethers. My first official speaking engagement was canceled.

> *The country was crumbling, but I had been working hard, and in the weirdest time, when so much was changing, and people were terrified, I reached one of my biggest goals.*

Early on, we could all feel the anticipation. Things were changing in our world that we had always depended on. You couldn't buy toilet paper. You couldn't buy paper towels, hand soap, dish soap, and other essentials. These were the little comforts we'd never thought about and had always assumed would be there. That's when I started thinking, *Wait, are we gonna be okay?*

The country was crumbling, but I had been working hard, and in the weirdest time, when so much was changing and people were terrified, I reached one of my biggest goals.

I'd ordered my Lamborghini the week COVID-19 hit, and it was coming. It was too late. I couldn't stop the delivery. I'd already paid my deposit, and the car was on the truck being delivered. It was weird because everyone was getting furloughed or laid off, and I was getting a Lamborghini.

I almost felt guilty. The country's situation made me feel like I couldn't be proud. I didn't want to be ashamed, but I was. You didn't necessarily see me out on social media. The timing was all wrong, and I didn't want to be construed as, "Hey, I'm out here reaching my dreams while you can't eat." It would have been in bad taste. So COVID-19 stole some of my thunder when I bagged a huge accomplishment I'd wanted to reach that dated all the way back to my childhood. (My brother Johnny and I had a poster of that very car when we were kids.)

So, I kept my new car under wraps, but I went hard on a new door-to-door sales program that my company was going to launch. A film crew followed me around to show people what it was all about. We had drones, and I was wearing a prestigious GoPro product as I went out executing. The program was designed to teach people how to increase their business and drive door-to-door sales in any industry. I was demonstrating that it worked in our roofing industry. To get into the program, people had to invest $500-1,000. Then, because of COVID-19, it all went flat.

People weren't investing in their businesses, and no one was sure they would even have a job. Then, by the grace of God, Dallas, Texas, considered roofing, construction, and remodeling essential. Yes, I do believe that was God favoring me again. I was more than a little fortunate, and I know that.

When a few storms rolled through, business picked up. People's roofs were leaking, and they needed our services. In the back of my head, I thought, *It can't get any worse.*

We'd just had a baby girl, Pepper, when all of this was going down. I looked at our new baby and our other two daughters and told myself, *You do not have time to feel sorry for yourself.*

We were going to thrive, or we were going down—along with everyone else. My instinct was to refuse to fail, and push forward.

At that moment, as I stood there and regarded every one of my beautiful girls, I decided to do exactly the opposite of what other people were doing.

I doubled down on my business and marketing.

When everyone was pulling back, I talked to my marketing team about pivoting. We'd all been ramping up marketing, building a website, and everything else that goes on when you are launching something new. I knew people were pulling back on marketing, but I also knew proprietary information. Some of the other roofing companies had pulled all their marketing. I figured if no one else was out there in the market advertising, I could get more of the market share.

I'm a calculated risk-taker because I trust myself and use the information at hand to move forward, embracing the risks. Because I had built up my business beforehand and had stacked a solid pipeline, I was in a financial position that could have allowed me to take the rest of the year off if I so wished or *needed*. I could have let off the gas pedal, but that would have gone against everything that I've ever talked about. I'm not one to sit around and wait to see what happens. I'm built for something bigger than that.

When they canceled school, we had to pivot again. My wife started teaching gymnastics to our oldest daughter, Coco. I was trying to juggle everything at home because, at the end of the day, I want to always protect my family.

It's my job to keep everyone calm. I was running a business, expanding it, and protecting my family while everyone was out buying guns and ammunition.

Meanwhile, fake news only stirred up the state of the world.

I heard it. I listened to it, and then I really leaned into my schedule. We sat down as a family and said, "This is what we're going to do." We kept as much of the old structure as we could. We committed to continue to eat breakfast and dinner together. When Coco didn't have school, we did online learning and got the Wi-Fi, iPad, and every other tool set up so it would work. Even though we had to adjust again, it was okay.

Then suddenly, the gyms shut down. It was time to buy a treadmill, so our fitness didn't drop off. At the very least, I could do my cardio wearing a weighted vest while walking. I also got a pull-up bar and refocused on bodyweight exercises. I took my exercise regimen completely back to the basics. I adjusted.

People kept talking about getting "the COVID-19." But they didn't mean the virus: They meant gaining 15-19 pounds from stress-eating all their COVID-19 snacks. It was a joke (but it really wasn't).

> *I went against the grain again and determined that I would get in the best shape of my life— no crazy snack eating for me.*

I went against the grain again and determined that I would get in the best shape of my life—no crazy snack eating for me.

And just like that, I did get into the best shape of my life. Instead of going to the store, my family and I had groceries delivered to our home. I got hooked up with ICON meals (a healthy meal delivery service) because I still wanted to eat well. Since my food was delivered to the house, I had no room for excuses.

My business expanded 38% over last year's numbers, and that was without a hailstorm. I doubled my numbers—during COVID-19—the biggest, worst global pandemic the world has seen.

In addition to lighting a fire under my existing business, I started a new company designed to disinfect homes and businesses. I wanted to be on the frontline of opportunity. So I made an investment and bought several ozone machines that create high levels of O3 and disinfected homes. I created a team whose mission is to go out daily and disinfect offices because that's the new normal. My business filled a public need. You can do the same!

Life has been better than ever in certain ways and weirder in others.

ACHIEVING IN HARDSHIP

This is the perfect time to talk about introducing the Six Assets of Alignment into your life. When you are searching for certainty and stability, having a routine and a purpose are incredible tools.

This is also the perfect time to examine where you're at with your faith. If you are freaking out right now, the nice thing is, as long as you have faith, you know that everything is going to be okay.

There's also an advantage to hunkering down with your family. A lot of families now had the opportunity to reconnect. Kids weren't going to school. Parents were 'stuck' at home spending more time with their kids—YES, it was wildly hectic and bizarre—but it was also so beautiful. No one had predicted *this* opportunity!

Lots of people were furloughed. Many companies tried to do the 'right thing' with the Paycheck Protection Plan, but a lot of people's finances were up in the air. I was saving money, but I was also investing heavily to gain market share in my industry.

I watched as the people in my network had issues with work and even within their own companies. My network was pulled away from having in-person meetings, but, thankfully, we could stay connected virtually. I had to think outside the box when it came down to my personal business and production.

I'm in some car groups, and it turned out many of those members' homes were in need of some work. Some had leaking roofs. Others had remodeling projects. At that exact point, my network became part of my net worth. We're all still referring business to each other, which is very cool.

And let's not forget about the book you're holding in your hands. This is a stand-alone book packed with the best life and business principles you'll find anywhere—*and it was produced during a worldwide pandemic!*

I am in a place where I experience nothing but positivity. I don't allow myself to get distracted by fake news. The reason I didn't go crazy was that I didn't settle for less. I didn't back down. After everything I have been doing for the last ten years, it was time to step on stage to perform. It was my time to shine and prove to people that this is what I was born to do.

On the heels of my mindset shift came the importance of being mentally sound. What really reared its ugly head during COVID-19 is that some people were trapped, unable to connect and spend time with their loved ones.

Also, during this time, suicide rates went through the roof. A lot of people took their lives, and, unfortunately, more will. People found out that they manage stress differently. Domestic abuse increased, as did child molestation. We can't ignore the dark facts of this pandemic and those individuals who are in danger. The devil is in depression and anxiety, and he surfaces in times of extreme strife.

I consider myself a highly functioning depressive person—I acknowledge that. I've battled depression. I have anxiety. Although I've been diagnosed, I choose not to use medication because I don't feel like numbing out or that turning off certain receptors in my brain is optimal for me.

When you feel trapped, depression is going to sneak up on you. Wherever there's doubt about your life, it creeps in. Then we tell ourselves, *I knew this was going to happen. It was too good to be true. The market was too good. The economy was too good. Life was too good.* In such odd circumstances, lingering depression is going to show up. Make sure you plan for it.

If you feel depressed, go dig a huge hole outside. You cannot be depressed and do hard work at the same time. It's physically impossible for your brain to operate like that. Of course, digging a hole is an analogy. All you have to do is keep busy, but I don't necessarily mean with monotonous busy work. What you do has to be structured.

Physical fitness releases endorphins in your body, which creates a happy feeling like you have achieved something big—and you have. Go after wins. When you wake up, count all the things you're grateful for. Consume positive messaging, whether through a podcast or an audiobook. Stop watching the news—all you'll see is negative press. That's because bad news makes the news more often and is more compelling than good news.

I can't control COVID-19, but I can make sure that I have a stronger immune system through my physical conditioning.

Experts say that COVID-19 attacks your respiratory system. Well, guess what? I'm going to be okay. If I were to get COVID-19, it would be no match for my health regimen. I take vitamins. I eat well. My health, fitness, wellness, and mindset are my armor.

Here's another odd fact about being on a schedule. If you stick to it, you'll feel freedom in it. I was operating and still following my system, and I thrived.

[
What I am telling you works. I am living it every day, and every single day I feel that I have it all.
]

What I am telling you works. I am living it every day, and every single day I feel that I have it all.

Even now, in the midst of a global pandemic, I can say I feel that I have it all.

Don't think it's possible? Still skeptical? All I'm asking is that you remain open to improving. Just start by believing that your life can change. Let what you are reading really sink in.

I did it. I am living it, and I will say this next part over and over again until you believe it—you can, too.

Don't forget the question you asked yourself earlier: *Why not you?*

List all the reasons that you can succeed in achieving the biggest dreams in your life.

You might write down that you have great network connections, that focusing on what you want to do will allow you to give up what you don't want to do. You can write about your plan to hold onto your self-confidence. This is a bit of a different take on writing a pros and cons list. This exercise forces you to only look at the positive in your life, as you brainstorm on how to leverage it to get where you want to go.

SECRETS OF ALIGNMENT

"A lot of the conflict you have in your life exists simply because you're not living in alignment; you're not being true to yourself."

—Steve Maraboli

I wake up every day and feel that I am behind. Maybe you expected to read something different. This isn't a scarcity mindset, but I use it to move the mountains of my day. My biggest fear is that I haven't lived up to my potential. I want my life to matter, to leave a legacy of what I value to impact my kids' and future grandkid's lives. I want them to know my core values, so they can live in a way that brings them joy, too.

I am thankful to have discovered the Six Assets of Alignment because even if I am struggling, I know I am reducing my pain by holding onto my control. I will always have a base, and so life won't get dark. It might dim a little, but the core confidence of who I am and how I am living outshines it. My values outshine it.

I am self-aware enough to make shifts when changes in relationships happen, which fills me with a sense of accomplishment, too. No matter what happens in my life, I want to show up to be the best version of myself that I can.

That's quite an accomplishment for an underweight little boy who grew up in a trailer park.

Yet even though I am far away from my childhood, I know my life today is also only the tip of the iceberg.

There is so much more. I am going to get it all.

Whatever I dream of and want, I know how to get, now.

And that is truly the secret of success.

Everything can be engineered.

Even success.

Now, you better buckle up because I am about to teach you that very secret.

APPRECIATION AND ALIGNMENT IN YOUR LIFE

While I am happy in the present and thankful for what I have and what I've achieved, I aim to lock down goals for my future and strive to make them a reality.

It's okay to do this. Regarding life in this way doesn't make you ungrateful—no matter what other people on the sidelines of your life say. It is possible to sit in thankfulness while also resetting your goals to go after bigger targets.

Goals are forever evolving around us, and it's up to us to move forward with them. It's up to us to shape our lives into what we want them to be.

Living your life in Alignment doesn't revolve around having money, either.

Yes, money is a piece of the puzzle, but it's just a single part of a grander picture.

I am also not insisting that you aim for perfection. We can all agree that's not a healthy goal. Besides, you won't ever get there.

[
You're better off striving for the best version of yourself instead of what you think is best.
]

You're better off striving for the best version of yourself instead of what you think is best.

I've had to work on that particular way of thinking and have learned when you finally accept it that it makes up a huge component of feeling as if you are living life to the fullest.

It is definitely up to you to reorder your priorities and reassure yourself of what you need in life, but, maybe more importantly, attention must flow to what doesn't matter. Where are we in our relationships, in our jobs, with our kids? What are we putting effort into that we don't need?

Often, when we aren't happy with where we are, we think about how we can have a different existence. Our hunger revolves around what we don't have—and this can be any old thing that doesn't matter. We get fixated.

If you think back on your life, you'll probably agree that most of the time, we try and maintain our creature comforts versus refusing to go to work. We try to have good relationships versus the alternative, etc.—unless addiction or self-sabotage is involved. We do generally seek to improve ourselves, even if we go about it the wrong way.

DEFINING YOUR "WHY"

The reason we make any decision in life comes down to two motivating factors: pain and pleasure. But inside those two factors is one more question that you need to consider when you think about the decisions you have made and will make—*Why do you make the choices you do?*

My biggest 'why'—and you can have several—is to do my best and to be the most successful for my girls. Let me tell you: It took me a long time to dial that one in. I was confused for years.

So, if you are still trying to figure out your 'why,' that's okay, for now. As we go through this chapter, you will get the hang of it.

By the time we get to the end of the book, knowing your 'why' will be nearly subconscious.

When you find out your 'why,' you can leverage it to unlock your personal power. Knowing exactly what I do and do not want has helped me identify my 'why.' I suggest that you take the time to figure out the same.

In this chapter, we are going to define your 'why,' and we are also going to connect it to those two motivating factors—seeking pleasure or avoiding pain because it is all interconnected. I know it might be confusing at the outset, but please bear with me. I promise, when you get down to understanding the real reason you operate the way that you do, your decisions will shift.

> **As you live by the Six Assets of Alignment,
> you need to know whether you are seeking pleasure or
> avoiding pain as you work to reach your 'why' (your ultimate goal).**

As you live by the Six Assets of Alignment, you need to know whether you are seeking pleasure or avoiding pain as you work to reach your 'why' (your ultimate goal).

HOW THE SIX ASSETS OF ALIGNMENT CONNECT TO YOUR 'WHY'

Let me add another layer to this equation of living your best self and having it all. Let's tie everything we have just talked about to living by the Six Assets of Alignment.

I shared a great deal about them in the Introduction. If, at any time, you forget the gist of why these assets are critical to your journey, please refer to the last part of the Introduction to catch up.

Now, if you're keeping track, we have:

1. The fact that you are motivated by pain or pleasure.

2. That you must know your 'why.'

3. The combination of one and two should be implemented into living the Six Assets of Alignment.

But here's another important question: Do you love winning, or do you hate to lose?

These items are all interconnected. You could not pull them apart if you tried.

To help you better comprehend this concept, let me use an analogy to which I think you can best relate to.

When you take your car into the mechanic to get an alignment, the mechanics put it on an alignment rack, and using a laser and other equipment, they get the tires aligned, so they are all pointing in the same direction. If a tire is not in alignment, the inside will wear out faster. On a normal tire, you might get 25,000 miles, but if something's out of alignment, you're going to get only 5,000, and then the underlying belts will show. Not only that, but you will pull your car all over the road as each tire fights with the other to be the one in charge of where you are going.

If that tire takes on additional wear and tear and the tires represent the areas of your life that need to be in alignment with each other, but aren't, you have to realize that you are adding additional stress in certain areas of your life.

Conversely, if all four tires are aligned, driving down the road will be faster and far more efficient. Your tires will last longer and give you better value. The goal is for all parts to be lined up and working in conjunction with one another so you can go straight down the road.

> *You can move forward if you're out of alignment, but it's not going to be optimal, and it will take you longer to get to your destination.*

You can move forward if you're out of alignment, but it's not going to be optimal, and it will take you longer to get to your destination.

If everything's flowing in the right direction, your life is practically effortless.

So now that you know what it takes to get to optimal alignment, you've got to take the time to set it up. You've got to facilitate it, so it will happen. Alignment doesn't just happen magically. You have to identify the areas of your life that need to be aligned with each other.

What Lincoln said is a good standard for where to spend your time: "If you give me eight hours to cut down a tree, I'm going to spend six hours sharpening my ax." Aligning your life is no different. You've got to prepare. You can't head out blindly into your existence.

As you know by now, the way the Six Assets of Alignment work is that every day you have to put effort into six specific areas of your life: And each of them must be aligned to work with the others.

This concept I am teaching you has to do with where you need to put your time. You will check on these areas. You will make sure you touch them and work on them daily. When you do this, you won't have to worry about balance. You will be nurturing every area of your life.

I hit upon the strategy of living in alignment versus trying to balance everything because I started doing life wrong. I was robbing Peter to pay Paul: stealing from family time to give to my business and neglecting networking in favor of making excuses. I made a big mess in every vital area possible.

I want to be hugely successful, but I don't want to be a hectic millionaire because then I'll have a terrible family life. If I am scrambling and don't know where to focus, everything will be lopsided, and my wheels will point in all different directions. I will pull from my family, my business, my finances, my sanity—you see where this is going. And I had to stop myself because no way in hell would I put my girls through any of the neglect and pain I'd suffered.

I remember trying to live that way and thinking, *Man, this ain't it.*

So let me remind you, it's not necessary that every part of your life has to be equal. It just has to go in the same direction.

It takes work. I won't lie about that. To get done what you need to, you may have to get up earlier to spend time with your family. You may need to make more money to hire someone to clean the house. When you solve these problems, then you will have more time to spend with the people you love the most.

Everyone's trying to find their inner child, their balance, their center, but that's just nonsense to me. If you sit around ruminating about your problems, you're just going to manifest more problems. That's why I don't like the idea of AA or Al-Anon meetings where everyone talks about the problem instead of thinking about the solution.

YOU DESERVE IT ALL

Our whole life, we are told that we need to get real. We need to get serious, and even if we abhor what we are doing with our lives, we need to like it. But the truth is you deserve anything you want. You don't have to pretend to like anything. If you don't like it, stop what you are doing. Go after your 'why.'

> *If you don't think you are worthy, why not? In the wake of every high performer achieving their dreams, why not you? Why can't you have everything you want?*

If you don't think you are worthy, why not? In the wake of every high performer achieving their dreams, why not you? Why can't you have everything you want?

You can. That's the great news! You just need to be very deliberate about it.

When I grew up, I wanted more. I didn't and don't make a secret of that, but the replies I was given made me cringe: "Why do you want that?" "That's not going to work for you." "Why don't you focus on some goals you can reach a little easier?" Even at a young age, I felt that I deserved more. I sure knew I wanted more.

We're told to live small. Go to school, get a job, work in a corporation for 30 years, get a 401(k), and, hopefully, we'll have enough money to retire on for ten years.

But—then you're dead. That never made sense to me. *What about the rest of my life?* There's got to be more to it than that.

the rest of my life? There's got to be more to it than that.

I grew up completely impoverished and could easily play the victim. I could get down on my life and declare I don't deserve anything more than the very least, what I can get by on. I could insist, "I'm just gonna do drugs or alcohol and lean on that because that's my life, and I don't have any control over it."

I know too many people who have rolled over and given up on their lives.

Take a moment and envision where you would like to be in five years, in ten years, in 20 years.

1. Where are you living? Have you moved to a different state or country?

2. What kind of house are you living in?

3. Who are you living with?

4. What's the first thing you do when you wake up in the morning?

5. What do you eat for your meals?

6. How much money is in your bank account?

7. Who do you spend your time with?

8. What kind of car do you drive?

9. Do you have children?

10. Do you have pets?

These questions are another way for you to get in touch with your deepest desires in life, the ones we often ignore because we tell ourselves we have to play small, that we shouldn't waste our time, that we are going to fail. This is an exercise in envisioning your highest self. So don't leave any detail out. You have to see it before you can be it. That includes all the areas of your life that you want to work together smoothly, that you want to use to build on and enhance each other.

Do this, and you will find yourself in Alignment.

ACTIVATING YOUR ASSETS

"Don't wait until you are ready to take action.
Instead, take action to be ready."
—Jensen Siaw

Innovation is temporary.

The time to seize these opportunities I have shared with you in this book is **now**.

People run hot and cold. They'll go to a big conference and come back gung-ho, but then the excitement will wear off, and they will fall right back into what they do daily. They'll come home and don't do what they were all jacked up to do.

That's not going to be you, not if you've made it this far in this book. Not with the fire you have in your belly, along with the urge to do more and make more of yourself (and for yourself).

You've found the way: Now, you can't be afraid of the work!

I now know that I need to tie in my purpose with my goals, so my efforts will last.

This is the most effective way to stay on the right path and keep all your wheels pointing in the same direction.

You want to tie into the *'why.'* Instead of being completely self-centered, figure out how whatever you're doing is going to hold you accountable. Start with having a purpose.

Having a purpose makes you want to do the work because it is so meaningful for you.

In some cases, the compulsion to succeed will lead you forward. You will find you won't have to push yourself as hard to make time to complete the steps of your plan. That's the best-case scenario.

In some cases, the compulsion to succeed will lead you forward. You will find you won't have to push yourself as hard to make time to complete the steps of your plan. That's the best-case scenario.

SELF-IMPROVEMENT

Self-improvement helps me run a more efficient company, which helps create a better economy. I pay to take care of the families of the people who work for me. I'm making an ecosystem. If I'm not taking care of what I need to on a given day, a trickle effect ensues, and then the stakes are much higher. There needs to be a bigger picture and the right timing to maximize what you are doing and how you are helping other people. Combine this with your 'why,' and it will direct you down the road you want to go.

We also need to look outside ourselves to learn what we don't know. We need to be coachable and allow people who specialize in certain areas and even in micro-areas to help us reach new epiphanies about ourselves and our business.

When you go to a mastermind event or even join a mastermind group, you invest your time for a weekend or possibly the year! You spend the money, sit in your chair and soak it all up, and then you are *charged* with taking the steps that will maximize the lessons of the mastermind. *It's not enough to be a sponge. You have to wring the knowledge out all over your business and your life.* Talking about doing it and actually doing it are two different things that equate to vastly different results.

When I joined one mastermind group, in particular, I went through the motions for the first 90 days. And when I wasn't getting the results I wanted, I stopped and asked myself: *Why is my business not changing?* The answer was within me. I had to take a hard look at myself. I was not staying motivated, and I wasn't using the resources and tools that were needed for my business to grow. I realized I needed to dial in my focus and systematically work through what I had learned, and then I needed to pick out what worked from the recommendations I was using.

I use the knowledge of the people who have come before, so I don't need to reinvent the wheel. As I move forward, I know that I need to alter my methodology by making small changes to suit my life and business. I know I will need to improve processes so they can be used over and over again, which saves time.

If your business isn't running the way you want, ask yourself if you need to multiply tasks and break down each job individually. Think of the different ways that you can get over the hurdle in front of you. Handle what needs your immediate attention and delegate what you don't have time for or what you don't want to do (or don't do well) to someone else who loves the work and is an expert in it.

In other words, what is your highest and best use of resources and time?

REASSESS PERIODICALLY

Prioritize what's on your list to accomplish and add it to your timeline, but also find out what can be pushed off to the next week, not because you want to procrastinate, but because you are trying to work as efficiently as possible. As you work your way through your projects, it makes sense to reevaluate what deserves your immediate attention and what doesn't. Ask yourself if the world will implode if you don't complete a specific task that day. Is what you are intending to do going to matter five years from now, or even later in the week?

> *A part of being efficient is knowing not only what you should do, but when you should do it.*

A part of being efficient is knowing not only what you should do but *when* you should do it.

Don't be afraid to scramble things up to make the best use of your time.

As you operate, believe that you're taking complete ownership of your agendas. No one knows you better than yourself, so stick to what works.

TIME, OUT OF THIN AIR

If you have to work from nine to five, you're going to be at the office regardless. Why not create small competitions that force you to get as much done as possible? On a typical day, you'll likely go from 9:00 AM-noon in the first half of your day. That's a lot of time to make good headway.

Tackling a good chunk of your tasks in the morning frees up your afternoon to work on other creative outlets. In a sense, when you break your day up into two parts, you are working as if there are two days in one!

In your 'real' job, or even if you are hustling on the side, you'll want to know the answers to the following questions so you will be on point:

- How can I outwork the competition?

- How can I gain a competitive edge?

- How much productivity can I create?

- How can I make things interesting, so I don't burn out?

- Do I feel burned out, or am I just bored?

If you're in a nine-to-five job and are not an entrepreneur at the moment, you're being paid for your time. So you need to create ways to make your job interesting or see about taking on different projects. Doing this might even help you nab a promotion! You'll definitely stand out more. On the other hand, as an entrepreneur, time isn't always conducive to money.

We all have the same 24 hours in a day. How was Steve Jobs able to create Apple when he had the same amount of time as you? Let's not discount that his fierce drive likely saved him time. When you love what you do and are compelled to do it, you get good at it because you choose to do it. You are spending time to improve—you are vested.

When I was 15 years old, I got a part-time job at a country club and I had experiences just like those you see in the movie *Caddyshack*. I was caddying at the same country club where Jack Nicklaus learned to play golf.

It was a pretty incredible place. What an eye-opening experience for a kid from the West Side!

The golf course opened at 7:30 AM, and as a caddy, you had to be there at 6:30 AM so that you could get on the roster and in the lineup.

I figured if I could get to the course by 6:30 AM and start my day, I could see my friends at the end of my shift. They all wanted to sleep in and then go to the pool for the rest of the day.

But I got up early, rode my bike, bummed a ride, or whatever I could do to get to the golf course. I never had my license in high school, but I'd be at the golf course and, usually, would start a round of golf by 7:30 AM. Then I'd be done by 11:30-noon, but I had anywhere from $80-150 in my pocket while my friends were still waking up and pouring bowls of cereal. We would all chill at the pool for the rest of the day. The difference was that I had $150 in my pocket that they didn't. I was making effective use of my time.

When I was 19, I got a job as a janitor in a bingo hall. I was paid $10 an hour each time to clean this miserable, filthy hall. It was so disgusting it could have been a nuclear waste plant, with the amount of cigarette smoke and the number of ashtrays it always had. I worked hard and put my head down to get the place clean in two and a half hours. That also meant I didn't get the $50 average anymore. I got $25, even though I'd done $50 worth of work in a shorter period of time. I got so proficient and cleaned so well that I cheated myself out of more money.

Here's another odd way to beat the clock: Get validation from yourself. Then you don't have to tick away the minutes seeking validation from other people when you should have been looking inward, to begin with. That's major *mindset* and confidence work. Stack the deck as you go with what makes you feel confident. Looking good (working out), feeling good (eating well), being productive (following a plan for your goals), achieving wins, adding support to your network, giving back, spending quality time with those you love and who love you in return, etc. Whatever it is that you need to do to build your inner confidence, do it, and you will spend less time seeking opinions from irrelevant people. You simply will not care about others' opinions after a while because you will gain your own self-confidence. When you have low moments in your life when implementing this new self-validation, you will not even consider anyone else's opinions. Only yours will matter. You will stop comparing yourself to people and will accept that where we are in our lives and in our goals can vary.

The moment you start validating your accomplishments and what you can do will be the moment you will step into your true power!

EXCELLENCE EVERYWHERE

Do you see the common thread in everything we have talked about in this book? We are striving to do everything as efficiently as possible. Whether you are finding ways to make money, attacking a new project, making up your mind, or meeting new people, you can save time when you get specific about what you want.

Once you start writing out an accountability schedule of what your day holds and sticking to it, you'll be amazed at how much your productivity goes up. In an accountability schedule, you would include all the calls you have scheduled that day, anything on your calendar that needs attention (doctor's appointments, etc.), any project that has a deadline, time for working on projects to move them forward, time with family and friends, personal time for meditation or prayer, time for learning a new skill (like how to invest), errands you need to remember to run, people who you need to connect with (personal or pleasure), your kids' extracurricular activities, time for relaxation, and so on. Include all aspects of the Six Assets of Alignment, and you will be astounded at your productivity.

That feeling of accomplishment will blow your mind once you feel it for the first time. It's a snowball effect, motivating you to want to do more. Before you know it, you'll be thinking, *Wow! I got all this done today! Now, what else can I do?* Yes, even exhaustion will take a backseat to prodding yourself to seek more excellence.

While holding yourself accountable, if, for some reason, tasks are not completed as planned, you'll ensure to tackle them first thing the following day because you will have conditioned your mind to always win. It doesn't matter if you don't feel motivated, are tired, or even if you want to be lazy. You'll know you need to get the work done, and you'll do it.

Use the accountability schedule and watch your excuses disappear. Pretty soon, the more action you take, the fewer the excuses you will make, and before long, they will become a thing of the past! Your mind will be so quick to shut them off that you won't even entertain not sticking to your plan.

You'll also realize that no longer are you the person who says it's everyone else's fault. If you look at the life of people who pass the blame and the buck, you'll note they have financial, marital, and relationship issues.

These are the exact people you want to get away from.

If you want to really blow your own mind, combine using an accountability schedule with another trick I learned...

MAKING MONEY

In the fall of 2003, I found myself beginning a fresh career in new home sales. I had the best schedule ever, working from 1:00-8:00 PM. Everyone told me, "Yeah, dude, we go out every night, sleep off our hangover until like 11:00, and then we're good to go." These guys were making about a quarter of a million dollars a year, and at 21 years old and newly hired, I took it all in. *That could be me.* I couldn't believe it.

But I knew that drinking and partying every night wasn't the path paved for me – not in an elitist way or anything like that. It was just my time to set forth and start my climb upward. It wasn't long before I realized my new schedule was allotting me quite a bit of downtime. So, I got a part-time job originating loans.

I woke up early, made calls, refinanced people, did option arms, and made crazy money. Then at noon, I would grab lunch and be in the office to sell new homes until 8:00 PM.

I made $33k in my first month in the mortgage business—significantly more money than I was making at my real job.

While the other guys were sleeping in or nursing a hangover from the night before, I was up and moving—exercising and then originating loans, all before I showed up to my full-time job.

Here I was again: *Using time to make things happen. But now, I was making serious money, too.*

I did eventually get fired from my new home sales job when my boss found out I was originating loans. He said it was a conflict of interest. (It didn't matter that I wasn't doing loans for the houses I was selling.)

Looking back, I know now that everyone around me was just jealous that I was doing well. They saw my name on marketing around town. I was working hard and reaping the rewards of my efforts. It's an unfortunate yet helpful lesson to learn: Sometimes, people will not be happy for you, and they will try to bring you down. (That's okay—you just keep moving up.)

CARRYING YOURSELF

Persistence is my superpower, and it's yours, too. That, combined with being a dreamer, is how I was able to get through the hardest times of my life and figure out where I needed to go and what I needed to do to get there.

Looking back, I simply had the belief that one day my life was going to be the way I wanted it.

I know now, sometimes that's all you need. Hope can be the first step you take to move out of your situation.

When I was younger, people told me, "You carry yourself well, like someone much older. That's pretty cool." I don't know why I carried myself differently or even where I learned it. Maybe it had to do with the fact that I was undersized and had a chip on my shoulder, which made me feel a little tougher than most. Maybe it was because I squared my shoulders and looked people in the eye. When I did that, I felt confident and in control.

The other thing I learned as a kid was to always do my best no matter the circumstance. Anytime I tried a new sport or did something different at school, I strove to be the best. I didn't learn this mindset: It must have been imprinted in my DNA, and I kept at it. When I played Little League Football and was only 50-60 pounds, I strode onto that field like I could kick every other kid's ass. I knew I ought to fight hard and hit harder so as not to get smeared on the grass.

Now, I hold my head up, accept my gifts, and I never allow myself to forget where I came from. I worked hard to leave that life of misery and abuse, and I am damn proud I survived it.

I shared the story of my childhood because you need context. You need to understand that you are not crazy for reading this book and listening to what worked for me. We all have tragedies in our lives. We all have horrible moments that define us. I am now thankful for what I went through and know with 100% certainty that I would be a different person without my past. I have chosen not to be a victim of those things that happened to me. But it was how I decided to move forward that was the difference. Many people will find themselves stuck because the story they keep playing in their minds will hold them back and not allow them to move forward.

If you change your story, you'll change your life!

Now, do yourself a favor and write down your defining life moments. Then take a minute to give thanks for what you have been through and that you survived.

What I have shared with you in this book is not a gimmick, fad, or short-term trick that you only do for a short period of time. The Six Assets of Alignment is a lifestyle that needs to be embraced 100%—so you can have it all.

The Six Assets of Alignment are all you need to master your life. This system is not complicated, but it is effective. Every day I keep challenging myself in these areas, and my life keeps improving, even when I think it can't possibly improve anymore!

> *Going through these assets is not a matter of reaching a destination. No, you are on a lifelong journey. Get your feet wet, and then practice, practice, practice.*

Going through these assets is not a matter of reaching a destination. No, you are on a lifelong journey. Get your feet wet, and then practice, practice, practice.

You will need to work the hardest at your mindset and being nimble with your positive self-talk, in knowing and reinforcing what you will tolerate.

When you take care of these Six Assets of Alignment, they will take care of you. Suddenly, you will worry less because you are following a program. You will feel more loved and cared for.

You will love harder and more deeply. You will believe in yourself more than you ever have and see yourself win every day. You will feel better, have fewer money issues, look better, think clearer, and have a deeper understanding of your purpose.

That has been my reality, and I hope it will soon be yours.

Let me recap the most critical takeaways that need your attention in the Six Assets of Alignment before you turn the final page, so you are clear on how powerful this system is:

1. **Mindset** – People are wired to search for long-lasting solutions, but the challenge is that life is unpredictable. We really don't have the control that we think we have. Much of the time, we feel that the circumstances of life come at us all at once, leaving us without any choice but to just react. Using the Six Assets of Alignment allows you to be proactive. When you decide to take care of your mindset—in the form of practicing positive self-control, meditating, refusing to seek outside validation, seeing challenge as a learning experience that can only improve your life, and learning how to flex the part of your brain that controls panic, procrastination, and anxiety—you will achieve anything you want. I like to remind myself that I am in control of my perspectives. I can get down on myself when things take a turn I didn't expect, or I can use moments like that as an opportunity to learn how courageous and powerful I can be. We have the most personal growth during life's most challenging times: It's all in how you perceive it. Use these times to galvanize your mindset because you'll be prepared the next time you are faced with a similar problem!

2. **Faith** – So many people choose to cling to the idea of a bigger power without understanding what they are putting their faith in. They give up what little influence they have and shut out any form of self-belief. It is time to be honest with yourself and learn to cultivate faithful moments in your life, like using prayer to clarify decisions, committing to accept the truth of situations to more effectively manage them, surrendering to a greater power or force, even if all that means is making a promise to be open to what you don't know, to seeing signs that can inform your direction. Having faith can be one of the most calming experiences of your life. It can be a regular part of everything you do. It can fill you with the belief that you don't have to be alone in making the hardest decisions. It can embolden you to strike out on new paths. I encourage you to remain willing to learn from your faith and to shed your ego to get there.

3. **Family** – They are the people we love the most. They also want the most from us. Sometimes, we may grow to resent this, but that comes in part from feeling we are letting them down when we strive to hit the impossible work-life balance. Family can be the people we include in our closest inner circles. A family born of blood or choice—it doesn't matter. And we all know that a life worth living isn't one that is only filled with work. It is one where we know we are doing our best for the people we love

the most. A huge component of knowing we have done our best for our family is loving them the way we want. When we do this, that nagging voice telling us to drop what we're doing and spend time with our kids and spouse fades away. We also learn that it is easier than we think to connect with people in a meaningful way. We all do have 20 minutes to read a book with our children or an hour to take them to the park. We do have the time in our day, but whether we find it or not depends on our priorities. My daughters are my number one priority. If I work all the time to take care of them but never see them, there is no point to my life. Learning to include family more means choosing differently, but with the Six Assets of Alignment, family becomes an immediate, valuable, and rewarding piece of your existence every single day.

4. **Fitness** – I hate to say it, but we are all growing old. That enviable metabolism slows down that we all flaunted in our twenties before we knew that a leaf of lettuce could bring on five pounds. As I stated earlier, a part of the reason I work out is that I don't want to go back and do the work to lose weight and go from fat to fit, as I laboriously did with my trainer back in the day. If I keep up what I need to do and make sure to hit the gym like a habit, then my road is easier. I will enjoy better health. I will feel better. I won't struggle to fit in a time to get to the gym that feels unfamiliar because I will already be in the habit. Entrepreneurs and business owners need to be as healthy as possible to keep up with the changes in the market. Working out creates endorphins, clarity of thought, and it gives you the stamina to pursue greater ideas and more innovations. Do what works for you. But do something. Work out at least once a day to build your energy. Stop eating a specific junk food and then build on eliminating more unhealthy foods from your diet. Pledge to sleep more each night and really follow through. Every day, approach your physical fitness with the mindset that you are giving yourself a gift.

5. **Finances** – It can feel so tempting to buy stuff we don't need. A deep inner urge hits most people, telling them to prove to themselves that they are worthy, that they are doing a good job being a provider, and that they will not deprive themselves. We are all great justifiers whose bad money habits can cause the death of our net worth by a thousand little cuts. An Amazon spree here because "I had a tough week," and a new car there, when "What? Am I supposed to work my whole life and never enjoy my money?" And many people eat their money, throwing it all at

the food apps that plague us now. It is easier than ever to spend money. And we are also surrounded by people who, if they are broke, want us to be, too—the human need to connect and be understood is that strong. But at the end of the day and your working life, you literally can burn away your savings. Using the Finances Asset means that you will learn to handle your money efficiently: You will nurture it every day. You will think of ways to maximize your gains and profits, so when it's time to splurge and buy your dream car or whatever is on your dream list, you'll be ready and appreciate it more!

6. **Network** – Our lives improve when we are careful with who we spend time with. This is an asset that deserves your undivided attention. This is also the area of your life that might give you the most pain. People, by nature, want to feel good. They want to please others, and so we aren't honest with what our lives need to get unstuck. We're not honest about the relatives and friends who seem to mean well but who demonstrate they are highly uncomfortable when we strive to get ahead and do more. Creating a network of people who cheer for you is exciting, but on the flip side, limiting contact with someone because they are detrimental to you is stressful. It is sad. It makes us feel guilty and as if we are judging people. But we aren't because we do have the right to choose what's best for us. When you commit to using the Six Assets of Alignment, you also commit to putting your relationships under a microscope and adjusting and eliminating the ones that are toxic. At the same time, you will stick to the new plan of meeting new people who share your passions and hobbies. I have found that the sadness at realizing the toxicity of friends and family members who must be addressed and potentially avoided is eclipsed by the relief of choosing different people to do life with. I know you will feel the same.

The only action left to take is to apply the Six Assets of Alignment to your life— and then do the work.

To make your life and transition into the Six Assets of Alignment even easier, I have developed a specifically designed app as a companion to this book. It will help you stay on track in meeting your goals.

This book was also meant to be a guide that you can return to when you need to re-read key sections to better manage your life. Use it in conjunction with the app to enjoy an optimal experience that will keep you on track to having it all.

Simply visit BurtonHughesOfficial.com to download the Align Your Empire app and get started Aligning your Assets and your life today!

ABOUT THE AUTHOR

Burton Hughes grew up tired of hearing the words, "That's not for you," that were so often uttered when he sought to escape his impoverished upbringing. He was a child who had endured so much that he had very little hope of getting out of his tragic and tumultuous environment. And the statistics were grim.

Witnessing the near murder of his mother, only to be thrust into unfathomable grief when he lost his older and revered brother – "stole his air." But the inner mettle and strength in Burton wouldn't die. He knew at a young age that he had a quality he couldn't yet identify residing in him. It was hope, and the relentless and deep knowledge that more was out there also gave him the push he needed to escape his old life and reinforce that he would finally decide what was for him or not.

Coupled with a never-say-die work ethic, fierce intellect, and literal model good looks, Burton wasn't comfortable with his gifts. Then one horrific day, he almost lost it all. His life hung in the balance. The lowest point of his life taught him how much he had to live for: that he was called to have more in life and that people were out there waiting for him to lift them up to find their own liberation and success.

Fueled by his discovery of the Six Assets of Alignment, Burton dismantled the logic of the work-life balance concept, instructing his clients instead in the art of aligning the six major assets of their lives most needing cultivation. The Assets of Mindset, Faith, Family, Fitness, Finances, and Network require varying levels of attention, according to the goal-plan devised. He lives by the Six Assets of Alignment every day and encourages people to follow his lead, knowing their own personal brand of success is waiting for them.

After implementing the Six Assets of Alignment into his life, he empowered himself to establish various businesses, modeled for multiple media outlets, and coached clients in reaching their elite life goals. He continues to strive for greatness every day.

Burton and his family, including his three adorable daughters, live in Dallas, Texas.

Align Your Empire is his first book.

For information on private coaching opportunities with Burton, please visit BurtonHughesOfficial.com.

DISCLAIMER

Much of this book is a truthful recollection of actual events in the author's life. The events, places, and conversations in this book have been recreated from memory. The names and details of some individuals or entities have been changed to respect their privacy.

The information provided within this book is for general informational, educational, and entertainment purposes only. The author and publisher are not offering such information as business, investment, or legal advice, or any other kind of professional advice, and the advice and ideas contained herein may not be suitable for your situation. Any use of the information provided within this book is at your own risk, and it is provided without any express or implied warranties or guarantees on the part of the author or publisher. No warranty may be created or extended by sales representatives or written sales materials regarding this book. You should seek the services of a competent professional before beginning any business endeavor or investment. Neither the author nor the publisher shall be held liable or responsible to any person or entity with respect to any financial, commercial, or other loss or damages (including but not limited to special, incidental, or consequential damages) caused or alleged to have been caused, directly or indirectly, by the use of any of the information contained herein.